CASHING IN
TAX FREE

CASHING IN
TAX FREE

YOUR ULTIMATE GUIDE
TO A TAX FREE RETIREMENT
USING 1031 EXCHANGE AND DSTs
(DELAWARE STATUTORY TRUSTS)

LESLIE PAPPAS
CCIM, LEED AP BD+C

Printed in the United States of America

ISBN Paperback: 978-0-692-58214-5
ISBN eBook: 978-0-692-58215-2

Library of Congress Control Number: 2015957886

Cover Design: Timm Freeman
Interior Design: Ghislain Viau

For Evelyn

Contents

Acknowledgments

I have two colleagues who were pivotal in moving my career in the direction of investment real estate. Two weeks into my real estate career, John Carman, my manager when I was a new agent at Coldwell Banker, Palo Alto, CA, had the brains and insight to suggest that I serve investors in my real estate practice. He saw my extensive background in banking from early in my career, and knew that I could succeed in making a difference for real estate investors. Ron Ricard, Director at Investment Property Exchange and wizard of 1031 Exchange, introduced me to the world of syndicated real estate and 1031 Exchange. He knew I could develop a full service practice helping investors sell local rental property and moving them into diversified, hands-off, institutional class investments using 1031 Exchange.

Thank you both for the immense impact you have made on my career and life. You are both very special men and I'm lucky to have met you.

Thank you to my teachers and mentors at the public schools in Sleepy Hollow and Tarrytown, NY; at Vassar College and at NYU Stern Graduate School of Business, especially Karla Michael, Judy Forrest and Susan Beers.

So much of what I was to become in the business world is the direct result of my first job after my MBA, which was with Citicorp in Manhattan. At 24 years old, I was taught to be inquisitive, thorough, creative, tenacious, and to always keep the best interests of our shareholders and customers at the center of my work. John Post, Jessica Sheinman, Aviad Broshi, Howard Stein, Larry Sussman, Jim Bailey, Naomi Levin and Darcy Walker, were my leaders and mentors. I will forever be grateful to you all. I credit you with much of the success I've had in my career. Each of you is a home run!

Several people helped me get started once I joined the syndicated real estate industry so many years ago, including Richard Zimmerman, William White, Trevor Gordon, and Louie Ucciferri. Thank you each, so much, for helping me learn the ropes in this industry.

Lastly, I had *a lot* of assistance with this book. Sara, Bree, David, Emily, Carrie, my sisters and Louie helped shape the book from beginning to end, and I'm very grateful for your insights, guidance, experience and skill. Louie Ucciferri acted as editor and provided lots of feedback that greatly improved the book. Ray Simmons made sure some of my analysis of tax issues was correct. Brandon Balkman of Mountain Dell Consulting and Tony Grego of ADISA were both very generous in providing me with some industry statistics. Adriana Olson of PASSCO, Warren Thomas of ExchangeRight, Brian Nelson of Nelson Brothers, and Declan Marmion of BlueRock Capital helped with photos of some recent syndicated real estate offerings. I couldn't have done it without all of you!

Introduction

Thanks for picking up my book. I spend a lot of time with my new clients educating them in the obscure world of syndicated real estate in which I work. I've written this book to try to put to print everything I could recall sharing with them over the many years I've been in the business. I take what I do very seriously. Every day, I help people make decisions about their future and retirement and help place major portions of their net worth in real estate. It's a serious topic. I want to be certain that my clients understand what they're doing with their money. Truly, I take as much time as they need to educate them and help them feel a sense of safety in the decisions they make with my help and guidance. I figured it made sense to write this book and put my thoughts in one place.

The topic is straightforward: How to use investment real estate to develop a diversified real estate portfolio, capital gains tax-free, that is managed by experts, not you. When all goes according to plan, your portfolio spins off fairly healthy and predictable cash flow that is likely largely sheltered from taxes. Your properties appreciate over time, and if there are any loans on your properties, some pay down of loan principal will likely occur. Your properties will be sold in five to seven years on average, and you are in total control of the properties you purchase for your portfolio from start to finish. You buy new properties without paying capital gains tax on the old ones you sold. It's possible that your heirs will never be required to pay all the capital gains tax accumulated over your years of ownership, because the burden of those capital gains taxes will disappear when you pass away, under current tax law.

Does that sound nice? It sounds nice to me. So now you have the picture from 10,000 feet. Time to dig in and read the book. There are a few important things to keep in mind as you read it.

I wrote this for the everyday person. It's not a scientific treatise on Delaware Statutory Trusts (DSTs) or 1031 Exchange. It's not a scholarly piece. I don't use jargon at all, and wherever I introduce unfamiliar terms, I explain their meaning. That's why I don't have an appendix listing new terms to memorize or an index. My examples are in almost all cases very simplified, leaving out complicated aspects of the tax code and legal requirements of DSTs. The examples used in the book are roughly correct, giving you an understanding of the overall outcome of a particular case, but not analyzing every detail of calculating depreciation, for example, or other minutiae not relevant to your understanding of the concepts presented. I tried to make it an easy read, not a thick technical manual.

So what is a 1031 Exchange? A 1031 Exchange is a tax procedure written into the IRS code since 1921. A 1031 Exchange allows you to defer (not pay) capital gains tax when you sell an investment property as long as you reinvest the proceeds into other "like-kind" property held for investment purposes. There are specific deadlines and other factors to consider that will be discussed in Chapter 2.

What is a Delaware Statutory Trust (DST)? It has nothing at all to do with investing in the fine state of Delaware! DSTs are a legal structure that allows smaller real estate investors to access larger, institutional grade properties by contributing their equity along with a group of other investors. DSTs are offered and managed by firms that perform myriad functions on the investors' behalf. The benefits of DSTs for an investor include "hands off" management, pre-packaged financing (which the investors are not responsible for and do not need to qualify for), annual net cash flows currently in the 5%–7.0% range, potential appreciation, depreciation (tax shelter), the ability to close your purchase within a few days, no closing costs, and professional, national class management. DSTs are part of the syndicated real estate industry, and are also explained in Chapter 2.

Every investment in which I place clients is regulated by the Securities and Exchange Commission (SEC.gov) and the Financial Industry Regulatory Authority (FINRA.org). The syndicated real estate industry is a very heavily regulated industry, and that's for good reason: it protects investors. In our contact with investors, and in the investment materials we present, the SEC and FINRA insist on fair and balanced use of language. For a benefit, present a drawback. Be fair and honest. It's really quite simple. Throughout the book, I use case examples and present the many benefits and some drawbacks of DSTs. In an effort to write a readable book shorter than 150 pages, I have placed a list of DST investing risks in Appendix I. Please be sure you look at it a few times as you read through the book.

In a nutshell, there is a chance that you can lose whatever you invest. When new clients ask me how much they could lose by investing, I tell them a story. Imagine you own a duplex and out of the sky comes a giant meteor that takes out your entire property. All that's left is a very big, very deep hole in the ground. That's how much you could lose. It's a bit dramatic, but it gets the point across more swiftly than Appendix I.

CHAPTER 1

Investing in Real Estate:
What They Never Told You

Meet Jack and Liz Walker. They're a nice couple, the sort of folks who are easy to be with and always quick with a joke. The Walkers have owned a single-family house in Silicon Valley for nearly thirty years. It was the first house they bought together, and back in 1989 when they made their purchase, it cost a whopping $75,000.

In the intervening years, Jack and Liz have done quite well. They've flourished in their careers: Jack as a consultant, Liz as an industrial engineer. When they decided to start a family, they went looking for a bigger house. In the mid-1990s, they moved into their dream home and began renting their first house out to tenants. They vacillated between loving property management and hating it—Liz liked tinkering with things around the house, and Jack enjoyed fraternizing with the tenants. But after their first son was born, the Walkers found they were no longer quite as tolerant of panicked 2:00 a.m. calls from their tenants about a leaking pipe.

Today the house is worth $1,500,000 and has $1,400,000 in equity, subtracting roughly $100,000 for closing costs. Because Jack and Liz don't have a loan on the property, the rent they've been receiving is a nice addition to their monthly income. But as they plan for retirement, they realize there might be better ways to increase their monthly cash flow.

Against the $1,400,000 of equity in the property, the annual pre-tax cash flow return on the house is under 2 percent. At first this doesn't bother Jack and Liz—"It's real estate," they say, "you can't have everything." But if they had $1.4 million in mutual funds earning 2 percent, it's safe to say they'd be pretty unhappy. As they design their retirement income to travel, visit family, and hedge against inflation and medical costs, they recognize that 2 percent cash flow for what it is: miserable.

Cash Flow = (Annual Income-Annual Expenses) / (Market Value of Property – Loans)

So what do Jack and Liz do? They come see me.

Under my guidance, the Walkers sell the Silicon Valley property and execute a 1031 Exchange that protects the entire gain from capital gains tax (more on capital gains tax later). With the $1.4 million they realized, they invest equally in four different properties:

1. 2.5 percent of a Class A, garden style, 300-unit multi-family apartment property in St. Petersburg, Florida, from which they receive 5.5 percent projected first year net cash flow and a tax shelter of roughly 70 percent from depreciation;

2. 3.0 percent of a Class A, luxury, 250-unit multi-family apartment property in Nashville, Tennessee that yields 6.0 percent projected first year net cash flow and a tax shelter of roughly 80 percent from depreciation;

3. 2 percent of a one year old Class A 350-unit multi-family apartment property in Colorado Springs, Colorado with a 6.5 percent projected first year net cash flow and a tax shelter of roughly 75 percent from depreciation;

4. 2 percent of a large, centrally located retail shopping center in Dallas, Texas with 7.0 percent projected first year net cash flow and a tax shelter of roughly 80 percent from depreciation.

If those numbers mean nothing to you, don't worry: they will. By the time you finish this book, you'll know exactly what they mean and why they matter. But for now, suffice it to say that the each of the properties in which Jack and Liz invested are valued from $40 million to $100 million, and the Walkers own a partial interest in each.

The properties are institutional-grade real estate—the same kind of real estate that pension funds, real estate investment trusts (REITs), insurance companies, college endowments and foundations buy for their own investment portfolios. Instead of the 2 percent cash flow they were getting in Silicon Valley, the Walkers are now receiving an average of 6.25 percent projected cash flow after all expenses in year 1.

Every five to seven years, on average, the properties are sold, and Jack and Liz continue to build their portfolio and cash flow by executing additional 1031 Exchanges. Once again they've avoided the tax on the sale, and use the money they've earned to move into more property. They keep what would have been paid to Uncle Sam over the years in taxes within their estate, and earn additional income as a result.

The example below shows you the cumulative effect of how Jack and Liz's equity would grow over time if they performed 1031 Exchanges every five years into new properties, and if they didn't utilize 1031 Exchange at all. In the right column of this example, Jack and Liz pay capital gains taxes on each property sale and then reinvest in new properties. In the middle column, they utilize 1031 Exchanges for every property sale and subsequent purchase. If Jack and Liz are smart and take advantage of the tax code, they will perform 1031 Exchanges with each property sale and grow their equity to just over $2.9 million over twenty years. If, however, they decide they want to pay capital gains taxes with each property sale, their equity will only grow to $1.7 million. The difference, $1.2 million, is the positive effect of 1031 Exchange. All the details for this analysis are shown in Appendix III.

EQUITY BUILD OVER 20 YEARS WITH AND WITHOUT 1031 EXCHANGES

SELL OLD AND BUY NEW INVESTMENT PROPERTY EVERY 5 YEARS	PERFORM 1031 EXCHANGES	DO NOT PERFORM 1031 EXCHANGES
YEAR 1 CASH INVESTMENT (PROCEEDS FROM SALE OF HOME)	$1,400,000	$1,002,500
YEAR 5 PROCEEDS AFTER SALE	$1,683,669	$1,144,689
YEAR 10 PROCEEDS AFTER SALE	$2,024,815	$1,307,046
YEAR 15 PROCEEDS AFTER SALE	$2,435,085	$1,492,430
YEAR 20 PROCEEDS AFTER SALE	$2,928,484	$1,704,108

ASSUMPTIONS:

START WITH EQUITY FROM JACK & LIZ'S RENTAL HOUSE SALE
50% LOAN-TO-VALUE ON EACH PURCHASE
APPRECIATION RATE 3%
COSTS OF SALE 5%
TAX RATE 30%
REINVEST ALL PROCEEDS FROM PROPERTY SALES
BUY TWICE AS MUCH PROPERTY AS PROCEEDS AFTER EACH SALE

Jack and Liz have taken their one house they bought for $75,000 in 1989 and increased cash flow, diversified, and eliminated the late-night calls. They've set up a self-perpetuating hands-off system that is both a real estate investment play and an estate planning strategy. By systematically growing their estate, they're putting themselves on solid ground in retirement and leaving an ever-increasing portfolio of properties to their family.

Liz and Jack Walker are more successful than they ever dreamed. Not only are they no longer worried about having enough money for their golden years—they're fully prepared to savor every minute of it. They are a hypothetical example, and their situation is very similar to those of many of my clients.

What You Never Knew
You Never Knew

If you've picked up this book, let's assume you own rental property. And if you're like most of the people I meet who fall into this category, you're likely unhappy in one or more ways.

The spectrum of unhappiness is wide. Maybe you're sick of managing troublesome tenants or making constant repairs. Maybe you bought a duplex twenty years ago for $100,000, and now it's worth $1.0 million. You know that the property should be making you higher cash flow, but

PRE-TAX CASH FLOW ANALYSIS
CURRENT RESIDENTIAL PROPERTY VS. DSTs

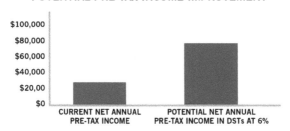

$32,782	CURRENT NET ANNUAL PRE-TAX INCOME
$78,000	POTENTIAL NET ANNUAL PRE-TAX INCOME IN DSTS AT 6%
238%	POTENTIAL IMPROVEMENT IN ANNUAL PRE-TAX INCOME

POTENTIAL PRE-TAX INCOME IMPROVEMENT

$100,000	
$80,000	
$60,000	
$40,000	
$20,00	
$0	

CURRENT NET ANNUAL PRE-TAX INCOME   POTENTIAL NET ANNUAL PRE-TAX INCOME IN DSTs AT 6%

SOURCE DATA ANNUAL—ESTIMATES	BEFORE TAX
RENTAL INCOME	$100,000
HOA	$0
INSURANCE	$2,500
GARDENING	$1,800
LEGAL AND PROFESSIONAL FEES	$500
MAINTENANCE AND REPAIRS	$8,000
MORTGAGE PAYMENTS	$28,368
PROPERTY TAXES	$15,350
UTILITIES	$8,700
MISCELLANEOUS EXPENSES	$2,000
DEPRECIATION ALLOWANCE ESTIMATE	$15,333
ESTIMATED SALES PRICE	$1,800,000
MORTGAGE AMOUNT	$500,000
EQUITY	$1,300,000
CURRENT ANNUAL INCOME RATE	2.52%
POTENTIAL ANNUAL INCOME RATE	6.00%
CURRENT NET ANNUAL INCOME BEFORE TAX	$32,782
POTENTIAL NET ANNUAL INCOME BEFORE TAX	$78,000
POTENTIAL IMPROVEMENT IN GROSS INCOME	238%
ORIGINAL TRANSFER PRICE VIA ASSESSOR	$1,150,000
ORIGINAL TRANSFER YEAR VIA ASSESSOR	09/16/09
DEDUCTION FOR DEPRECIATION ENDS	03/10/37
AMOUNT OF IMPROVEMENT VALUE VIA ASSESSOR	$460,000
ANNUAL DEPRECIATION ALLOWANCE FOR 30 YEARS	$15,333

you don't want to risk losing the tenants by raising rents. Perhaps you think rental property is a nuisance, but worth it because you're getting substantial appreciation.

Most of the people who see me think they're getting pretty good cash flow. They're not. They're getting miserable cash flow. Perhaps they have 25–75 percent of their net worth sitting on an earthquake fault line or in "Tornado Alley," and the "BIG ONE" could come any day. These people might be getting 1 to 2 percent annual cash flow from their \$1–\$2 million sitting in the ground. At best that's \$40,000 a year. At worst, \$10,000, and that's before taxes.

I can help these people, and I do. That's my job. Once I start working with an investor, I typically triple their cash flows. After taxes, I can usually quadruple them. But before I can do that, they have to acknowledge they have a problem. They've made the smart decision to buy and keep property that has appreciated handsomely. While they may not have done anything wrong, what they don't know can hurt them. They often don't know of 1031 Exchange, and few have ever heard of DSTs.

People speak of investments as high yield, low yield, or somewhere in between. They're also categorized as safe, risky, or somewhere along a spectrum. Mutual fund companies, stockbrokers, and financial advisors talk about the balance between safety and returns. When we step outside that frame of reference searching for higher returns or other options, we find the matter of active versus passive management becomes increasingly relevant—particularly in the realm of real estate.

Many people invest in real estate, either in addition to traditional investments or as an alternative. But they quickly discover that potential attractive returns come at a personal cost. For an individual investor, real estate can be a high-risk, undiversified proposition—and a high-maintenance one, too. The calls about the faucet leak, or the broken air-conditioning, or the plumbing backing up inevitably come at the most inopportune times.

Your investments must fit into your life, both the life you have and the life you want to have in retirement. If family is important, if travel is important, if freedom is important—your investments shouldn't intrude. **I suggest you Invest to Live, Don't Live to Invest.**™ There's a whole wide world out there, and to miss it while you babysit real estate is a shame.

And yet, we don't want to leave real estate off the table— the returns are too attractive. Real estate usually provides tax shelters too. It's an extremely valuable investment, *in the right context*. The key is to move away from the high-risk, undiversified, high maintenance single-family residence, duplex, fourplex, strip mall, small office, small multifamily apartment, retail, land or "Triple Net" (NNN) properties and explore something different. Sophisticated investors can access a higher level of real estate, a level with historical returns that for some firms have averaged at or above 9 percent per year over the last 2-4 decades. Below are examples of overall returns from some of the firms with which I work. These figures are the average of all properties that each firm has bought, operated and sold for their investors.

Internal rate of return = [(total pre-tax cash flow) + (appreciation) + (pay down of loan principal)] / (number of years held)

FIRM	AVERAGE ANNUAL INTERNAL RATE OF RETURN
COMPANY A	9.0%
COMPANY B	13.0%
COMPANY C	18.0%

These results were provided by each firm. Past results do not predict future results. Returns are not guaranteed, as in any form of real estate investing. All investments, including real estate, involve risk. This is neither an offer to sell nor a solicitation of an offer to buy securities. The information on this page alone should not be used in making investment decisions. The prospectus is controlling. Investors should carefully consider the investment objectives, risks, charges, and expenses associated with any investment.

Six Strategies for Owning Rental Properties

There are six key strategies to maximize return from real property. For this discussion, we'll focus on large-scale multifamily apartment properties to bring the six strategies to life.

1. First and foremost is **property selection**. It doesn't behoove you to own one, two or three properties in one town or county. Non-diversified real estate is risky. It's particularly dangerous if your properties are all in one geographical area that is supported largely by one local industry, like technology or the military. This lack of diversification can be particularly cataclysmic in an area like Silicon Valley, where I am based. As I say to my new local clients: not only are you not getting enough cash flow; half of your net worth is sitting on the San Andreas Fault, in a town with only *one industry*. And when that industry falters—because it will—it's going to affect the economy of the whole area. If the city, county or industry suffers substantial changes, your $2 million house can easily become a $1 million house seemingly overnight. Talk about a seismic shift!

It's much safer to spread your $2 million over multiple, carefully selected geographical locations and varied types of real estate than to keep one high-value property. Remember Jack and Liz? They didn't reinvest in just one property; they reinvested in four. And they avoided Silicon Valley entirely, choosing four other prosperous and growing submarkets of large cities. When you diversify, your properties will be spread out all over the country, in towns with multiple industries, above-average population growth, and above-average income growth. Any of these factors lowers your risk—combine all three and you've got a winning strategy for lowering risk.

2. The second strategy is **active property management**. Some people love managing their investment property. They enjoy fixing the toilet, installing the smoke detectors, and mowing the lawn. They want total control. For others—and in my experience, it's the majority—managing the property is a necessary evil. A tenant leaves after ten years, and it's time to break out the checkbook and put $10,000 into the property, hire contractors, go through re-tenanting, and hope the next tenants pay the rent and don't trash the place.

The "**Five Ts**"—toilets, tenants, trash, taxes, and termites—can be exhausting. Horror stories abound. Tenants take the toilets, pour concrete down the sink, kill the landscaping—all on a $1,000 deposit. You're left trying to get blood from a stone.

In institutional property management, professional managers oversee several institutional scale properties at the same time. These professionals have decades of experience and a track record of selecting, managing, and maintaining property and generating solid return on investment. Their job is to maximize income and minimize expenses.

No matter how much energy and time an individual devotes to being a good manager, she can't do what an institutional class, professional management company can. After all, most people who own rental property also have full-time jobs! Below market rents aren't adjusted higher, expenses aren't tightly controlled or usually even budgeted. Both of these actions—or inactions, as the case may be—can severely reduce cash flow. They may also limit potential appreciation.

You don't have to manage anything—you just have to get the right people in place. Active Property Managers keep their finger on market rents and bid out the vendors annually to curb expenses.

3. The third strategy is to explore **secondary income streams**, such as rental washer/dryers, pet fees, storage room fees, and the like. The land your property sits on is not the only asset you can monetize. But without the requisite knowledge to set up secondary income streams, most people won't even consider it.

4. The fourth is **property maintenance**, the kind that garners great reviews via word-of-mouth and various rating websites. If your property is well maintained, you'll have tenants lining up to move in. But if property maintenance is usually done only on a tenant phone call, the relationship with the tenant will inevitably suffer.

5. You must also keep **tax implications** in mind, including avoiding capital gains tax with tax-favored transfers and maximizing depreciation. Taxes are often left to the accountant after the fact, and because some tax advisors

aren't adequately equipped to navigate these kinds of situations, owners typically end up gifting the government with significant overpayments. The tax implications of selling an investment property can be devastating, and the fear of it often keeps people from selling at all. *Capital gains tax will take 15–40 percent of your gain* when your property is sold. This level of taxation can make it very difficult to keep the cash flowing so you can continue to build your estate.

LONG TERM CAPITAL GAINS TAX RATES FOR MOST ACCREDITED INVESTORS (1)

TAX ELEMENT	RATE
FEDERAL (2)	15-20%
STATE	0-13.3%
DEPRECIATION RECAPTURE	25% OF DEPRECIATION CLAIMED
MEDICAL SURTAX	3.80%

1. Some of these rates are based upon tax bracket and/or income.
2. Taxpayers in the 10% and 15% tax brackets pay no Federal Capital Gains tax.
This table is roughly accurate, but not a full representation of the tax code.
To understand your specific situation, please consult with your tax advisor.

A more advanced real estate investment strategy uses 1031 Exchanges—the same strategy Jack and Liz Walker used. You don't need to have a background in tax law to understand how it works: Just know that 1031 Exchange allows you to defer taxes when you sell one property and soon after buy other investment property. That means you don't have to carve out a chunk for Uncle Sam; you can invest the entire amount you earn. There are procedures and technicalities we'll discuss in Chapter 2, but you can see how saving 15–40 percent in taxes can substantially increase your ability to build your estate and improve cash flow. By using a 1031 Exchange, you no longer have to be afraid that by selling an asset, you're giving away a large portion of your profit to the government.

6. Last but not least: **maximize cash flow.** If you don't consider cash flow, and the only significant return on your investment is appreciation, you are leaving a lot of money on the table. What if an earthquake *does* sink Silicon Valley into the Pacific? In that nightmare scenario, you can kiss your appreciation goodbye. But if you find ways to maximize cash flow, it brings in valuable cash *now* instead of far in the future via appreciation. Some ultra-conservative investors will evaluate the worth of a potential real estate investment by whether or not the total cash originally invested can be gained back during the hold period *just from cash flow,* not counting any appreciation.

Those are my six strategies; strategies I've used time and again with my clients to move them from a place of frustration to a place of improved after-tax cash flow and better quality of life. If you're feeling overwhelmed by all the information, don't worry—it's completely natural. Who has the expertise, time, and bandwidth to accomplish all these things simultaneously anyway? This explains why many people in individual real estate investments are doing what is known as "coasting."

Each strategy presents a unique challenge—and a tremendous opportunity for growth. Advanced-level investment in real property not only captures financial benefits in each of these areas; it solves many of the issues that keep people out of the real estate market. It also eliminates the problems and fiascos that current investors are keen to escape.

Mastering the six strategies is a way to shift the paradigm. It's everything they never told you about real estate—and exactly what I'm going to teach you in the following pages.

Accredited Investors

In this book, I'll outline how to move from having a "coasting" real estate investment to a diversified, institutional-grade real estate portfolio. We'll discuss the six strategies in greater depth, as well as the attendant benefits you can expect to experience. But first a quick word about who qualifies for this kind of investing.

The Securities and Exchange Commission (SEC) is the federal agency in charge of enforcing securities laws, proposing rules, and regulating the securities industry. It has a three-part mission: to protect investors; to maintain fair, orderly, and efficient markets; and to facilitate capital formation. All investments are governed by the laws, rules, and regulations of the nation and the SEC, but the SEC makes a distinction between the regular folk and those whom they deem "accredited investors."

Accredited investors have a net worth of at least $1 million (not including the value of their primary residence) **OR** have had an income of at least $200,000 each year for the last two years ($300,000 combined, if married), with the expectation of making the same amount or more in the current year. Accredited investors have access to investments not available to those who don't meet these SEC criteria.

Currently, accredited investors make up about 8.25 percent of the US population. The SEC has delineated a small and exclusive club on the assumption that, due to their financial success, these people will be able to judge and participate in more sophisticated offerings as seasoned investors. Accredited investors are the only people who qualify to purchase the properties described in this book.

Investing in real property doesn't have to be hard, but it does require the acumen and skill set to make strategic choices and deploy proven strategies that work. In this chapter, I've laid out the basics of how a cohesive system of investing in institutional-grade real estate investment works, and why it's so powerful. In Chapter 2, I'll go into more detail about what it means to be an accredited investor with access to institutional investments, and the many options available to you.

My goal is to fill your toolkit with specific tools to help liberate you from hands-on property management while still making a handsome profit. If that intrigues you, please read on.

CHAPTER 2

How It Works: Entering the World of Institutional Investing— The Way the Big Dogs Invest

Institutional investing is a big word for a small concept. At its core, it is investing just like institutions—pension funds, real estate investment trusts (REITs), banks, hedge funds, insurance companies, university endowments and foundations do. These types of institutions invest in large-scale projects, unlike your average investor, who typically owns condos, single family homes, and 2-4 units (together referred to as residential 1-4 units throughout the book). Institutional investments are available to smaller investors under certain guidelines, i.e., accredited investors from Chapter 1.

Without pooling funds with other investors, individuals generally don't have the ability to invest in larger, more attractive properties that have the potential for returns not typically possible at the residential 1-4 unit level. These investments typically range in scale from $20 million to $100 million or more in value, and are the opportunities we'll discuss in this chapter. We will focus on multifamily apartment DST investments throughout the book, as most of my investors find this category of commercial real estate easiest to relate to. My experience is that multifamily apartment investments provide the best after-tax returns while also being the least volatile of all real estate segments, so it makes sense to focus on them for examples in the book.

In the syndicated real estate market, where institutional scale investments are made accessible to individual investors, firms called "Sponsors" offer DSTs for your investment. Sponsors acquire institutional grade property, package it into a DST legal structure, usually get financing on the property, offer it as a straight cash or 1031 Exchange investment to accredited investors, and manage the property on behalf of the investors until its ultimate sale. In a DST, the Sponsor has an obligation to manage the property toward its highest financial benefit. However, the investors own the property. Eventually, when the Sponsor sells the property, the investors will have gained whatever cash flow, appreciation and pay down of loan principal the Sponsor was able to achieve. Depreciation allowance will help shelter annual income from taxes.

How and where you invest has utmost importance because your investment funds represent years of hard work, discipline and effort, especially if they came from investments in smaller properties such as residential 1-4 units. Your property was rented and maintained. You kept it in good shape and did everything you could to maximize the return. When it's time to move into a different investment, you are looking for a vehicle that will meet and build on that level of care.

Sponsors do much the same thing, but on a larger scale and with a level of experience and professionalism residential 1-4 unit investors don't have—think Little Leagues v. the Major Leagues. Sponsors typically have decades of highly specialized experience and employ specific methodologies over and over to acquire, manage, improve, and sell properties for maximum cash flow and profit.

Here's how it works. A Sponsor typically acquires one or more institutional-grade properties of a similar type, packages them into a DST legal structure, and offers them to accredited investors through securities professionals called registered representatives or investment advisors. Sponsors manage the DST on behalf of the investors. You, the investor, are the actual owner of the property. But instead of being on your own, you're now backed by a Sponsor with decades of experience, history, and financial savvy—a virtually priceless package.

There is great benefit for you to join hands with these professionals and allow them to put your hard-earned money to work. Let's break down exactly how Sponsors practice their trade and how it differs from what we can accomplish on our own in residential 1-4 unit investments.

How They Do What They Do

Sponsors have specific criteria, developed over decades of practice, on which they base their selection of properties to purchase. Some of the criteria may include plans to improve the use of the property. The geographic location also plays a large part in the selection criteria. Sponsors often source the properties off market using private relationships, and Sponsors seek to acquire property below appraised value.

Most Sponsors in the multifamily apartment market buy Class-A property— high quality, newer buildings with top amenities, higher-income earning tenants, and low vacancy rates. The properties are typically in secondary markets and sometimes in primary markets. Rather than New York City, L.A., San Francisco, or Chicago, they look to submarkets of major metropolitan areas such as Atlanta, Colorado Springs, Phoenix, Las Vegas, Dallas, Austin, Raleigh and Nashville. Key criteria include investing in submarkets that are growing faster than the larger metro market in regard to income and population growth. Sponsors don't invest on a hunch or a feeling; they select markets and properties that they believe will be profitable by using objective criteria developed over many years.

Sponsors tend to specialize in specific types of real estate and obtain deep knowledge in one particular sector. One might focus on retail, another on multifamily apartment or student housing, another on commercial office, another on hotels, and still another on senior housing. They apply their specific brand of expertise to the properties in their sector by increasing their net operating income (NOI). This specialization and resulting expertise in one segment of real estate investing is the primary ingredient to providing solid and consistent returns.

The foundation of providing a solid and consistent return is to increase net operating income over the life of ownership. Net operating income is total income minus total expenses not including loan payments. There are just two pieces in the equation to control: income and expenses. Actions that either increase income or reduce expenses change the net operating income and provide more return for the investors. Sponsors manage both aggressively. Some additional benefit to the investors may be achieved via appreciation in the value of the property and pay down of loan principal.

Net Operating Income (NOI) = Total Annual Income – Total Annual Expenses (not including loan payment).

Sponsors look to increase income many different ways. In multifamily apartments, they survey market rents daily or weekly and often adjust the rental rate for new tenants and lease renewals on a daily basis. Computer modeling is frequently used to fine-tune rents relative to the competition. They search out additional sources of income such as pet fees, garage and storage rental, and enhancements such as valet trash pickup or utilities chargebacks. Sponsors institute programs and amenities to maximize the attractiveness of the property to prospective tenants and to retain existing tenants. Some examples include building a dog park, a business center or a gym; resurfacing the pool; new pool area furniture; a concierge service; barbecues; and holding resident functions to improve resident retention. Sponsors also pay close attention to the online reputation of the community. Social media is big today, and savvy Sponsors use this to their advantage. They maximize their online presence and employ tactics to get more likes, friends, and followers.

All these factors can add $20 to $200 a month or more to the income derived from each apartment. That increase, multiplied by roughly 300 apartments in a complex across the course of a year, can dramatically increase net operating income. That's how Sponsors can manage the income side, which is only half of the net operating income equation.

On the expense side, Sponsors minimize expenses largely through economies of scale. Vendor services are bid together with other large properties the Sponsor manages, and discounts are thereby achieved on expenses such as insurance, maintenance supply and contractors. Service contracts are normally bid out every year to secure the best prices, and each year the property taxes are reviewed and potentially appealed. Sponsors scrutinize all expenses carefully and ensure the property is nicely manicured and maintained, and depending on the size of the real estate, staffing may be reduced to cut costs.

This is by no means an exhaustive list of the ways Sponsors create value by increasing net operating income, but they are some of the most effective. You can see that the majority of these methods are not available to even the most financially adept individual investor. By virtue of who they are and how they operate, Sponsors are able to operate on a much higher and more efficient level across a wider scale than individual investors.

The Structure

Just as business structures like C corporations and LLCs move in and out of favor based on the current legal and tax climate, Sponsors have changed how their offerings are structured to take advantage of various tax, legal and operating benefits. Prior to 2008, most syndicated real estate investments were structured as Tenants-in-Common (TICs) with up to thirty-five individual owners (investors). Each of the owners had decision-making authority on major decisions, and moving forward required a majority or unanimous vote. Any loan on the property required all the owners to qualify. It was a system that worked, but it was unwieldy during the Great Recession, when property values plummeted everywhere. Some properties failed and others required loan workouts. Individual investors did not have the commercial real estate expertise required to manage these decisions and votes. Also, achieving consensus among many owners proved difficult at times.

In the syndicated real estate market today, Sponsors almost exclusively use Delaware Statutory Trusts (DSTs) as their legal structure. Individual investors each own beneficial shares in the Trust, but they have no decision-making authority or personal responsibility for the loan on the property. It creates a streamlined process where the institutional real estate experts, the Sponsors, are tasked with property performance.

Within the structure of DSTs, there are two teams of managers. The first is a Property Manager. They manage the property and implement the business plan developed for the property. The second is the Asset Manager, who watches the property on behalf of the investors as if they owned it themselves. Asset managers design the overall business plan, manage its implementation, and watch the local market for opportunities and threats. The Property Manager and Asset Manager may both be within the same company, or the Asset Manager may hire a large national or regional property management firm. The Asset Manager is always an employee of the Sponsor firm.

Communication with the Sponsor

The Asset Manager heads a department called "investor services" whose function is to interact with and provide information to investors. This department provides monthly or quarterly reports, holds quarterly conference calls with the investors to discuss property performance, answers investor questions, and prepares individual annual tax packages for the investors to pass on to their tax advisors. The investor services department is the point of contact for anything the investors require. Even in a DST, where the investor does not have voting control, he or she can speak directly with the Asset Manager in charge of their property, ask any questions, and offer their ideas about the property. Investors are welcome to tour the physical property both before and after they invest.

Selling the Investment

When you invest in DSTs, you must plan on remaining in the investment for the life of it, usually from five to seven years. Just as you've held onto your current rental property, this is a long-term investment. Depending on the local market environment during the ownership period, the property could potentially be held for ten years or more. The business plan, however, will require the Asset Manager to continually review the likelihood of a successful sale usually from the third year of ownership on. It is not part of any business plan to hold a property for ten years or longer. It may simply happen if market conditions are unfavorable to sell.

The Asset Manager makes the decision to sell a property. When that happens, investors receive their pro rata share of the proceeds and are free to make new, independent investment decisions. Individual investors may choose to cash out and pay the capital gains taxes due. If the investor does perform another 1031 Exchange to defer taxes, they can buy whatever class of replacement property they wish, including DSTs, residential 1-4 units or any other real estate held for investment purposes defined as "like-kind." On average, every five to seven years you're presented with an investment decision and can reevaluate your portfolio at that time to make adjustments as needed.

1031 Exchange

1031 Exchange was briefly presented in Chapter 1. Let's dive a little deeper to understand what it is and how it works in tandem with DSTs to make investing even more powerful.

A 1031 Exchange allows you to sell a property and reinvest the proceeds into other like-kind property held for investment purposes, thus deferring the capital gains tax. I like to call it "avoiding" capital gains tax at the close, and you'll discover how later in the book. There are some basic rules about how an exchange must be handled, as well as more complex ones, including the three-property rule, the 200 percent rule, and the 95 percent rule. The complexities of those rules, and adherence to them, are managed by a company known as a Qualified Intermediary (or Exchange Accommodator). The Qualified Intermediary (QI) holds your sale proceeds in escrow, advises you of IRS guidelines, and effectuates the purchase of replacement property for you.

1031 Exchanges are limited to "like-kind property," but the IRS uses a very broad definition. Like-kind property can include any kind of real estate held for investment purposes. You can sell a rental house and buy an apartment building or land, for example. All residential rental, retail, commercial, industrial and many other forms of investment real estate can be exchanged and invested in DSTs.

The power of 1031 Exchange is the ability to do it over and over again. As each property is sold ("relinquished property"), you don't pay the taxes due when you close your sale. Instead, you retain all the sale proceeds and reinvest them. No amount is carved off to pay taxes. If you invest $1,000,000 and make $300,000 when that investment is sold, the full $1,300,000 is available to reinvest in "replacement property." Now your rate of return and the income check you receive on a monthly basis is calculated on an investment of $1,300,000, instead of $1,300,000 minus capital gains taxes paid. Remember the chart of Jack and Liz's equity growing over time from Chapter 1? If you do this every five to seven years, on average, it's easy to see how your investment nest egg can grow.

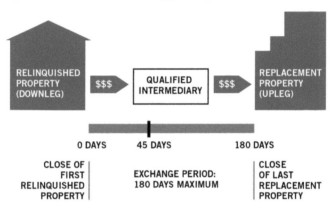

An important element to know about 1031 Exchanges is that you can reinvest all or just a portion of the proceeds of any sale. For example, Jack and Liz sold their single-family rental and received $1,400,000. They can take $100,000 out of the proceeds and remodel the kitchen at their personal residence or go on a trip around the world. They will pay capital gains tax on the $100,000 they've taken out for the kitchen or the trip, but the entire remainder of $1,300,000 can be used to reinvest through 1031 Exchange and avoid paying taxes at the close. This is called a partial exchange.

In order to complete a full 1031 Exchange, you must buy as much property as you sold and reinvest all of the proceeds from sale. This is the only way to avoid all potential capital gains tax due upon sale. If Liz and Jack in the example above had a $250,000 loan on the property they sold, they would need to buy $1,400,000 in replacement property and use all of their proceeds in the purchase of replacement property to completely defer all capital gains taxes. That means they would either need a $250,000 loan on their replacement properties or bring $250,000 in additional cash to purchase replacement properties. This is why most DSTs come prepackaged with a loan. In this way, investors can match their loan needs to the loans amounts available in potential DST replacement properties to avoid capital gains tax.

Whatever amount you desire to use for reinvestment moves directly from the escrow of the relinquished property to the exchange accommodator's escrow account. The funds cannot be transferred to your personal accounts, because if you "touch" the money, you will incur capital gains tax. The money will be held in the exchange accommodator's account until you make investment decisions and provide written authorization to move funds into one or more replacement property investments. You have forty-five days to identify in writing the properties you'd potentially like to buy.

Forty-five days can be a real time crunch for an individual investor looking to buy residential 1-4 units. You have to run around town viewing properties and gambling they'll still be available when the time comes for you to make an offer. You've also created a quagmire for yourself: plenty of time to worry that there are undiscovered issues that might make a property unattractive as an investment.

Time is much less of an issue with DSTs. There are generally a stable of suitable properties available and you can begin the selection process well before you close escrow on your relinquished property. You can begin to learn more about the various Sponsors and properties that interest you before your property actually closes sale. Most people will identify anywhere from one to five properties and buy several of them to diversify their real estate portfolio for added safety (see more on diversification in Chapter 5).

There is more information on 1031 Exchanges at http://www.archerinvestors.com, but you do not have to be an expert on 1031 Exchanges to use them properly. The key is to protect your money by making sure you're working with experienced, reputable people. A 1031 Exchange is only one element of the overall strategy of investing in DSTs. A knowledgeable professional can guide you to use them effectively, keeping your money safe and growing.

A Word About Costs

The subject of cost is one that every investor should thoroughly understand. In syndicated real estate, cost is referred to as "load." Properties are identified and purchased by a Sponsor, packaged as a security, and offered to investors through registered representatives or investment advisors. Built into the investment is a margin for the Sponsor, and the costs of putting together the investment offering, including commissions, legal, financing costs associated with the loan, marketing and other costs. Institutional investing is not philanthropic. Everyone in the deal expects to be paid for their investment in time, experience or equity, in the case of the individual investor.

Load averages 8 to 12 percent and is calculated based on the *cash invested*, not the entire purchase price of the DST. Some investors initially view load as a penalty. The thought is that 8 to 12 percent of their investment is going to disappear the moment the deal is done. In fact, load in DSTs is more analogous to the costs borne in all real estate transactions when acting as the buyer. Let's look at an example.

Riley is selling two properties worth $5 million to Emma. He has loans of $1.75 million. He pays a six percent commission to his agent and the buyer's agent, and one percent in other closing costs calculated on the selling price of the property. Riley spent seven percent of $5 million to sell this property, or $350,000.

Emma doesn't feel that she is at a disadvantage because Riley paid all that money in sales expenses. In actuality, if she bought the properties for $5 million, $350,000 of her payment into escrow covers the commissions and closing costs, however she doesn't think she's being taken advantage of by spending $5 million and receiving $4.65 million in investments.

When graduating to institutional investments structured as DSTs, the investor is buying a package of benefits that he or she could never access as an individual investor. Those benefits include participation in institutional grade investments, property selection, hands-off management, potentially higher cash flow before and after taxes, potential additional depreciation and appreciation, non-recourse loans for which the investor does not need to qualify, and many other benefits explained throughout this book.

Just like any other real estate, cash flow is calculated on equity investment. If an investor puts $100,000 cash into a DST, and the first year cash flow is projected to be 6.25%, the investor is projected to receive 12 monthly payments of $520.80, or $6,250 in the first year. The projected income is based on the full $100,000 equity invested.

The real key to understanding the costs of any investment is how long it takes to recapture the cost based on the projected rate of return. How fast will the investment get to a break-even point? Assume a Sponsor has historically returned 13 percent annually to investors, on average, over all their properties. The 13 percent internal rate of return (IRR) represents cash flow, appreciation of property, and pay-down of loan principal. If a DST investment tracks the roughly 13 percent historical rate of return in the first year, when compared to a 10–12 percent load, the investor will burn off the load before the first year is over. Few other investments can potentially burn off costs that quickly, and it's certainly rare in residential 1-4 units, unless you're flipping property.

Load is disclosed in the Private Placement Memorandum (PPM) for each offering and should be discussed fully with your advisor and clearly understood. A good offering incentivizes everyone to pull together towards the same goal to make it as successful as possible. Costs and commissions are just part of it. When you want to play tennis, you have to buy a racket, balls and sneakers—it costs something. The benefit is you get to play tennis. The benefit of DST investing is not only do you get to play with the big dogs; you get to be one of the big dogs.

The Lasting Benefits

DSTs remove the burden of property management and the **Five Ts**—tenants, toilets, trash, taxes, and termites. Much like we might hire a financial planner or money manager to manage our stocks, bonds and mutual funds, investing in syndicated real estate moves you to a place where other highly experienced professionals do the work for you. DSTs allow you to graduate up from smaller residential investments to institutional-grade investment properties. You'll partner with seasoned professionals having decades of experience. You'll leverage the power of economies of scale. And you'll maximize returns with business practices that individual investors cannot usually match.

Nelson Brothers Vue on MacGregor Student Housing DST, Houston, TX, shared Kitchen. Units range from studios to four-bedrooms, and are rented by the bed, not by the apartment.

CHAPTER 3

Guess Who's Coming to Dinner? Sponsors Are People, Too

S yndicated real estate investing is a longstanding but relatively obscure industry. It's not something you see in your local newspaper or on CNN—it is, after all, only available to the roughly 8.25 percent the American population who qualify as accredited investors. And yet it's certainly no newcomer to the investing scene in the United States. Institutional investing has been around for centuries—first as an esoteric idea, then in practice.[1]

Investing together in DSTs has many specific advantages that we discussed in the last chapter, and is the way an individual investor can graduate to institutional investing.

---

[1] http://www.investmentnews.com/article/20110327/REG/303279994

The History of Institutional Investing

Back in the late 1990s and early 2000s, leading Sponsors and real estate attorneys worked together with the IRS and established guidelines that would make the Tenant-in-Common (TIC) co-ownership structure clearly qualify for 1031 Exchange. TICs were the predominant legal structure used in syndicated real estate before DSTs. The text of the result, IRS Revenue Procedure 2002-22, is shown in Appendix IV.

As a result of Revenue Procedure 2002-22, the industry exploded in growth. Investors and their advisors had the Revenue Procedure to rely upon. If TICs followed these guidelines, they could qualify without question as "like-kind" property in 1031 Exchange. The industry grew until its height in 2007, when almost $4 billion of equity was invested.

Also in the early 2000s, the idea of the Delaware Statutory Trust (DST) gained traction. In 2004, a similar revenue letter was developed by the IRS that gave the same level of certainty to the DST structure regarding 1031 Exchange. In 2004, the IRS released Revenue Ruling 2004-86, allowing the use of DSTs to acquire real estate where the beneficial interests in the Trust would be treated as direct interests in replacement property for purposes of 1031 Exchange. This was another milestone for the syndicated real estate industry. IRS Revenue Ruling 2004-86 is what we now rely upon for our DST 1031 Exchanges, and you may read it in Appendix IV.

Then 2008 happened. I'm sure you remember it—and probably not with a pleasant wave of nostalgia. The Great Recession affected values of real estate across the country. All classes of real estate suffered, including TICs. As the banks became extremely conservative in their lending practices, TICs fell out of favor. In the TIC structure, banks review and underwrite each investor's credit worthiness, and because TICs can have up to thirty-five owners, banks found the work required to establish loans on TICs was simply too much to bother with. DSTs came into favor because lenders were willing to underwrite them. In DSTs both the property itself and the Sponsor are responsible for repayment of the loan. *Investors have no responsibility for the loan principal in the event of default.* This is called non-recourse financing to the investor. In addition, DSTs do not require that investors be credit approved by the lender. This advantage is also unavailable when investing on your own.

A few Sponsors still occasionally use the TIC structure, and their lenders are usually regional banks with which the Sponsor has a close and long standing relationship, and the burdens involved in underwriting up to thirty-five investors are acceptable because of their deep relationship.

The syndicated real estate industry has steadily come back since 2008. My personal experience with real estate investors during the recession was that they were unwilling to consider a different form of real estate investing and unwilling to sell property they owned, since they knew what to expect from those investments. The TIC and DST industry slowed dramatically from 2008–2011, but it steadily started to pick up as investors began selling investment properties again. Each year since the Great Recession, more and more investors have come back to 1031 Exchange as incremental normalcy came back to our economy. In 2015, the market rebounded to its pre-recession levels, and I was able to place as much equity as I did in 2007.

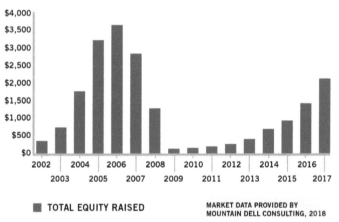

1031 MARKET—TOTAL EQUITY RATES MEASURE IN BILLIONS (SINCE 2002)

■ TOTAL EQUITY RAISED

MARKET DATA PROVIDED BY
MOUNTAIN DELL CONSULTING, 2018

Securities and Real Estate

Although the basis is real estate, because of its co-ownership nature, DSTs are considered securities, regulated by the Securities and Exchange Commission (SEC). In the industry's early years, many people with a license to sell securities, but with little to no real estate experience, entered the industry. Having previously sold only annuities, mutual funds or other securities products unrelated to commercial real estate, they placed investors into properties without a clear view as to how the investment would fit into the client's entire portfolio, particularly when it came to risk. Some also had little to no experience or education in real estate. Many poor choices were made, and many investors suffered. In addition, before the Great Recession, there were seventy Sponsors operating in the industry. Many were not well capitalized or did not have the depth of experience and talent that we see today in the roughly fifteen Sponsors still operating who made it through that horrible time.

Just as it is of utmost importance to work with Sponsors who have long track records and the best qualifications in their sector, the recommendations of particular investments by an investment advisor or registered representative requires the same level of experience and professionalism. Although DSTs are securities, at their core they are real estate, and real estate expertise and talent is a far more important skillset to find in your advisor than a traditional securities background.

The Legacy of Bernie Madoff

Bernie Madoff's legacy is a double-edged sword. Of course his actions were catastrophic for his victims, but on the positive side, as a result, we all tend to be more careful before making big decisions. We ask more questions of all our professionals, whether they are attorneys, doctors, or investment professionals. We do more research online and also ask for personal references and recommendations. We no longer write checks indiscriminately, especially when investing a large portion of our hard-earned money.

On the negative side, our trust has been compromised. We've become suspicious of the unknown, and Madoff's legacy has inserted a level of distrust between professionals and clients.

Vet the person with whom you're thinking of working. Go to their LinkedIn profile and read their history. What are their credentials? Is the advisor a real estate expert or a securities generalist? Does he or she have institutional real estate credentials, education and experience, or is he or she mostly managing client retirement accounts and other investment funds? How well does the advisor know the Sponsors? Does the advisor visit the properties they represent before you invest? Have they done the work necessary to know the property with a goal to protect you as well as they can? Talk to their clients and ask about their experience of investing in TICs and DSTs. Treat an investment professional like a doctor or an attorney, and investigate them. Know that most people you meet are not Bernie.

The DST Investing Leap

Investing in DSTs is a leap. It's different than traditional investing. I want our clients to be confident in and comfortable with their investments, and to that end I do several things that most other advisors do not. One is to take interested clients to a one-day tour of three leading Sponsors in the Los Angeles area. It's a long day, but the ability to meet three Sponsors, hear about their current and past offerings, meet their staff, and visit their headquarters gives my investors a terrific education in the industry and helps them develop better trust as a result. The reason a personal visit is so powerful is because it's hard to trust people you've never met. The education that results from the trip helps my investors make more informed decisions too.

I hold weekly online webinars with our approved sponsors each week. Every week, a different Sponsor is invited to come online into a meeting and present their strategy, track record and current offerings to my clients. Many of my clients find these webinars invaluable.

Another thing I do is invite investors to go see the properties they're considering purchasing. If you're going to invest in a multifamily apartment in Nashville, Tennessee and you're 95 percent sure this is the property you want, you can visit the property if you wish, and have a tour hosted by the Property Manager. The Sponsor will usually reimburse you for the cost of reasonable airfare, rental car and hotel if you end up purchasing the property.

Over the last several years, I have personally visited and evaluated almost every one of the properties I've recommended. If I haven't gotten on a plane, I've at least done a video tour. I travel a lot, and as I mentioned earlier, very few advisors work to protect their clients in this way. While it is not possible or useful for me to visit offerings of portfolios of properties (which can total over 20 properties each), if an offering is for a single investment property, which most are, I do the review. I either approve or reject properties based on my experience and education in real estate. I recently rejected a property because of its proximity to low-income housing, competing construction underway and vacant building lots. Those factors will likely limit the Sponsor's ability to increase net operating income or appreciation upon sale. The CEO of the Sponsor, a very bright man, personally called me to understand my position, but ultimately those factors meant I couldn't in good conscience recommend the property to my clients. That property did completely sell out, however. The advisors who placed client equity in that property were likely unaware of the adjacent low income housing, current competing construction and other lots nearby ready to be built on, all of which will possibly affect the property's performance over time. They didn't personally visit the property to evaluate its investment risk or potential.

Dinner at My Table

I also visit the Sponsors at their headquarters for a day of meetings. I evaluate their experience, competence and track record. I learn about their investment philosophies and strategies.

This is not an arm's length transaction for me. I require a high level of trust in the Sponsors with whom I work. My test is the dinner table—not any dinner table, but my dinner table. At the end of a headquarters visit, I ask myself if I would be comfortable preparing a meal for the people I've met that day in my own home. I suppose it's a gut evaluation of my confidence in their skills, my level of trust and my feeling of whether they are "good people" at heart.

I do the work to determine which Sponsors will be right to work with and which offerings I will agree to represent. That evaluation takes a lot of travel and time, but it means everything to my clients.

Passco Twenty25, Atlanta, GA, *is a multifamily apartment property that shows more like a private, gated community. The property was less than one year old when I toured it, and one of the best I've ever seen.*

CHAPTER 4

Who Can Do This and Who Never Will?

Now for a dose of pragmatism: DSTs aren't for everyone. Even if you *are* an accredited investor, DSTs may not be for you.

Even if a potential investor meets the SEC's criteria on paper, their financial advisor is obligated to take their entire portfolio into consideration to determine whether an investment is suitable. It can be a lively topic of debate between the advisor and client. For example, if a client's entire portfolio is invested in real estate and completely without diversification, the advisor is tasked with informing the potential investor that a sound portfolio strategy would be to cash out some of the proceeds of the sale and invest in stocks, bonds, and mutual funds, rather than to continue to invest in more real estate. Liquidity and a balanced portfolio are prudent; diversification is key.

For some, despite qualifying as an accredited investor, their personal cash position is weak. Putting their money into an illiquid investment for five, seven, or perhaps more than ten years may not be the right decision. It may be wise for them to perform a partial exchange, take $100,000 or $200,000 out of their transaction, pay the taxes, and give themselves a cash buffer.

The advisor doesn't make the final decision—the client does. The advisor is required to do what their name suggests: advise. They do not hold the role of enforcers; they merely make the determination of qualification as an accredited investor, provide investment advisory services, and in my case, offer clear recommendations regarding which properties to invest in.

The Age Factor

People fifty years of age and older are great candidates for DST investing. Certainly, younger clients have invested with me as well, however, people over fifty make up the majority of my clients. They've spent their lives building wealth brick by brick. They've been very active in locating, purchasing, and managing their investments. Here's how I typically see the decades break down.

In their fifties, I find that people are looking to spend their final working years making a big push on the career front. The effort required to manage real estate usually interferes with those plans. The opportunity cost is too high for them. I work with plenty of clients in their fifties who have invested in DSTs, whether they're still working or already retired.

In their sixties, retirement is upon them, and people have an added incentive to simplify their lives and enjoy the fruits of what they have built. They need cash flow to fund their retirement. In fact, cash flow trumps appreciation as the primary consideration in their real estate investments. For that reason, DSTs become even more strategically important. Also, in retirement, most people hope to work fewer hours or perhaps not at all, and being tied to rental property becomes less and less attractive.

People in their seventies and eighties are much the same, only more intense. The thought of one more late night "the toilet is plugged" phone call is beyond irritating. There is still time left for thoughtful investing, and the estate planning aspects of sequential 1031 Exchanges into DSTs are very appealing. We will cover this in detail in Chapter 7.

DSTs Aren't a Fit for Everyone

For all the benefits of DSTs, they aren't for everyone. There are some property owners for whom the "hands off" nature of DSTs is a negative instead of a positive. These investors generally have several properties and they enjoy managing them. They may have not have separate careers. They enjoy the details, and are active in obtaining the best possible return from their properties.

These hands-on investors like control. They don't invest in stocks, bonds, or mutual funds much, if at all, because they don't trust them. No matter how high the potential level of return may be, DSTs will never be a good fit. The lack of day-to-day involvement in DSTs is a deal killer for them.

DSTs are not investments where you get control. Just like when you invest in IBM, you have no decision-making authority except for an occasional proxy vote. You choose IBM because you believe IBM has a great business model, good financials, and/or great earnings per share along with the potential to grow those earnings. You trust that IBM is going to manage its business effectively.

Your control comes at the beginning, when you select your advisor, the Sponsors with which you want to invest, and the individual properties you will own. You trust the improvement, management, and business plan execution to the professionals.

Whether or not DSTs are a good fit is up to you to decide. With the help of a trusted advisor, you can explore the options and arrive at an educated decision.

CHAPTER 5

Diversification, Loans, and Depreciation

We've touched on the concept of diversification, loans, and depreciation, but I want to delve into these topics more deeply. DSTs and 1031 Exchanges are powerful tools, but they're even more powerful when combined with these three overarching concepts. We'll start with diversification.

Where Are Your Eggs?

As we've established, one of the big mistakes people make when they invest in real estate is to put all their eggs in one basket. They fail to diversify, either in terms of location, type of property, or management (worst-case scenario—all of the above).

Katie is a young screenwriter in Los Angeles. Ten years ago, her career really took off, and she decided to take her windfall of cash and invest in some real estate in the LA area. She was really smart to invest in real estate at such a young age. Katie now owns a small stable of residential properties that she manages herself. Not only are they all in LA—they're all within a two-mile radius. In Katie's mind, this is perfect. It means she never has to drive very far to attend to any of her properties. But lately it's been totally exhausting. She's thinking about delegating the day-to-day duties to a local Property Manager recommended by a friend.

Hers is a story of lack of diversification in action. Katie only has properties in one location. All the properties are 1-4 unit residential investments. She manages them all herself. She's put a lot of her net worth into undiversified investments. All it's going to take is one earthquake to reduce the nest egg Katie has worked so hard to build.

Think about it this way: you wouldn't invest all your money solely in Apple stock. If you really liked Apple stock, you'd buy some of it, and then diversify, buying stocks in different industries, and perhaps make another type of investment, like mutual funds. You would be sure you were well diversified. You would never put all of your money in just one place, so it follows that you shouldn't do it with your real estate either.

So what is diversification strategy in real estate? To me, it consists of three elements: **location, management, and type of property.**

Location, Location, Location

The issues with location are on display in Silicon Valley, my home market. We've already talked about the fact that all of the properties here are sitting on a major fault line. Not good. But just as detrimental is the fact that virtually every person in Silicon Valley depends on the technology industry, from the woman who does your nails to the attorney who guides you in estate planning. They all depend on the success of the local economy, and the local economy depends predominantly on the technology industry. In 2001 when the tech bubble burst, everyone in Silicon Valley was affected. You could literally look through the empty office buildings from front to back while driving down the highway. Every business took a major hit.

As a DST investor, you don't want to be invested in these types of areas. Even though these areas can *feel* very safe, diversification is essential to sound real estate investing. Think of the Old West ghost towns that were built solely on mining. Silicon Valley is the modern version, and not a good risk for all of your assets.

Invest only in communities with five or more different active and vital industries. Make sure no single industry dominates the local employment base. The more diversified the local industry is, the safer your real estate investment will be. If one industry fails or is compromised, the others will still support your occupancy and rental rates. Insulate yourself from the potential downturn of one industry. In my experience, the number one criterion for choosing property is to find a location with well-diversified industries supporting the local community.

One other important piece of the location puzzle is to select areas growing faster than the metro market average. Every real estate market has submarkets. Let's use Nashville as an example. Look at the growth of the specific submarkets in which you're considering investing. Is the population in the chosen submarket growing at a faster rate than in Nashville overall? In other words, are people moving to that submarket? Is the income in the submarket growing at a higher rate than the overall market? When investing in multifamily apartment properties, look for submarkets that are attractive to young professionals and retired people so that when the property is upgraded and operations and amenities are improved, the area will remain desirable and allow for increasing rents.

One more important element of diversification is geography, where the old adage "location, location, location" is quite literally true. How much can you mix it up? Don't invest solely in the Southeast. If you have two of three properties in the Southeast, make sure they are in different states. Your properties should be so different in their locations that no one event has the potential to be catastrophic. This is true diversification.

Management

In addition to paying close attention to location, you also want to diversify by Sponsor, i.e., management. When I'm helping a client research Sponsors to decide with whom they're going to work, I have a whole system of checks and balances in place to ensure they make the best possible decision. (We'll talk more about that in Chapter 6.) But I still prefer that my clients work with more than one Sponsor as yet another way to reduce risk.

Have more than one set of experienced people working on your behalf. Sponsors offer different talents, and each brings their own strategy to selecting, managing and selling real estate. It makes sense to get a good mix of strategic and management talent.

Type of Property

Syndicated real estate investing is found in many different types of properties with multiple subcategories. Each type of property has its benefits and drawbacks. Diversifying the types of property you buy is a terrific way to reduce risk and maximize cash flow. Properties are usually grouped into one of three categories: Class A, B, or C. These classifications are quite subjective.

- Class A buildings are considered the best in terms of quality of construction and location. They tend to be newer too.
- Class B properties might have good quality and construction, but with a less central or attractive location. They tend to be older than Class A properties.
- Class C properties are basically everything else.

1. **Residential property.** Multifamily apartment is my favorite asset class. To me, it's all about risk. It has the second lowest beta (volatility) of all the asset classes, meaning it goes up and down less in value, and it offers the highest overall returns over the past forty years when considering cash flow and appreciation. After all, people need a place to live.

PROPERTY TYPE CHARACTERISTICS
1978-2013

	MULTIFAMILY APARTMENT	OFFICE	INDUSTRIAL	RETAIL
APPRECIATION RETURN	3.2%	2.3%	1.2%	2.0%
CASH FLOW RETURN	5.9%	4.9%	5.5%	5.0%
BETA (1)	0.90	1.44	0.95	0.73

(1) Beta measures the sensitivity of an asset's total return to the market. Source: metlife.com/assets/cao/investments/US-CoreRealEstate-PastPresentFutureView_2013.pdf Originally sourced from NCREIF Property Index Data from Q1 1978-Q2 2013.

When we look at after-tax returns, multifamily apartment can provide the best annual cash flow of any real estate segment due to its shorter depreciation schedule of 30 years. All other categories of commercial property use a 40-year depreciation schedule. Residential also includes the subcategories of student housing and assisted living. These subcategories require very specialized knowledge on the part of the Sponsor, particularly assisted living. Assisted living demands that the Sponsor not only run the property, but run an entirely separate, regulated business too.

2. **Commercial office.** This category includes office complexes, office buildings, and medical offices. Medical office, in my opinion, tends to be the safest category within this segment, as doctors spend hundreds of thousands of dollars building out their offices and are less likely to move than other businesses. Physicians and other medical professionals tend to be more focused on their practices rather than continually seeking out the lowest rent per square foot in their local communities. Therefore, tenant retention is usually better in medical office than in other types of commercial office properties. Medical office becomes even safer when located coincident to a hospital.

3. **Retail.** This category includes shopping centers, strip malls, "Big Box" retail (such as Home Depot), and triple net properties (NNN). In DSTs, we also have

portfolios of Triple Net properties available. If you're not familiar with NNN properties, imagine Walgreens, Auto Zone, or Dollar Store. They are stand-alone buildings with one tenant. In true Triple Net, the tenant is responsible for paying property taxes, maintenance, and insurance (hence the NNN of Triple Net), and the property owner is usually responsible for the roof and walls. When we purchase NNN property, we like to have the corporation behind the retail store as our lease guarantor, not a franchisee. In this way, we can secure a lease backed by the assets of a major firm. That means lower default risk. Many people consider NNN investing with corporate-backed leases from multi-billion dollar companies to be the safest way to invest in real estate. It will also likely provide the lowest cash flow when compared to other retail opportunities. Retail can have higher returns than multifamily apartment, but also can present more risk. People need a place to live, but they don't necessarily need to shop. Adding some carefully chosen retail property to your portfolio can provide diversification to help lower risk. I often recommend investing a portion of your proceeds into a NNN portfolio for added diversification and as a core asset with relative certainty of income.

4. **Industrial property.** Industrial property is uncommon in DSTs, but it can be a strong category. Following the

same logic as medical office, when a business takes an industrial space, they are likely to modify the space to meet their specific needs with an assembly line or manufacturing equipment affixed to the walls, ceiling, and floors. Because of that large financial investment, they are less likely to move and interrupt operations.

5. **Hospitality.** Hotels and entertainment venues took the biggest hit of all categories in the Great Recession. I understand that hotel prices dropped in value during the Great Recession to the same degree they did during the Great Depression. During the recession, people and businesses simply stopped traveling, and they didn't start again for many years. In my opinion, hospitality as a category carries more risk than most of my investors are willing to accept. This isn't a Monopoly game—hotels are not the best investments for my clients, in my mind, purely from a risk standpoint.

The next chart shows you a distribution of the amount of equity available for investment among different property types in 2017 through December 29. Multifamily apartment makes up 60.0 percent of equity available for investment, while commercial office (16.0 percent) and retail (11.0 percent) dominate the remaining equity available.

AVAILABLE EQUITY BY ASSET TYPE

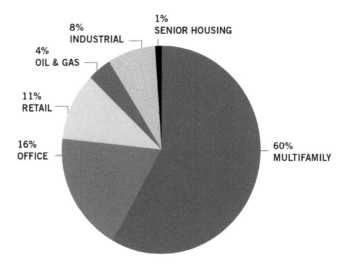

MARKET DATA PROVIDED BY MOUNTAIN DELL CONSULTING, 2018

The Tax Code Perks

The tax code is not easily understood, but investors can significantly increase their returns by fully utilizing the rules as written. The use of debt in DSTs can help improve return and lower taxes. Potential depreciation, as a deduction, is an important variable to consider in property selection. Utilizing loans and maximizing depreciation can significantly increase your after-tax cash flow.

Loans

You may recall from our discussion of 1031 Exchanges that under the tax code, you must buy as much in replacement property as you sold in the relinquished property in order to fully defer capital gains taxes. This includes equity and loans. The government uses these tax incentives to encourage investors to continue to invest and build a stronger economy. This rule of equal or greater investment becomes important when combined with an understanding of taxable gain.

Taxable gain is *not* how much cash you get from selling a property. Simplified, it is *what you made in appreciation by owning the property*. In order to calculate capital gains, we must first establish your "basis" in the property you are selling. Simplified, basis is what you paid for the property added to the cost of any improvements you made to it over the years you owned it. To calculate capital gain, we then subtract your basis from the amount you received in selling the property net of certain selling expenses. Your capital gain and the cash you receive from the transaction will differ, primarily due to loan payoffs to your lender, and/ or new loans taken over the ownership period. This means you could possibly owe as much in capital gains as the cash you receive, or even more, if you put additional debt on the property over the years you owned it.

Let's look at an example. Robert bought a property for $100,000 and now it's worth $1 million. He put $50,000 of improvements into it over the years by installing new windows, a new roof and remodeling the kitchen and bathrooms. His basis is $150,000. However, if at some point during the time he owned it, Robert took a $500,000 interest only loan against the property, he owes the bank $500,000 when he eventually sells it. His cash out of the sale will be about $430,000: $1 million minus the $500,000 loan minus about 7 percent in costs of sale ($70,000). His gain is the sales price minus certain costs of sale minus his basis (1,000,000 – $70,000 – $150,000). Robert's gain is roughly $780,000. Robert will have $430,000 to pay the capital gains tax on $780,000 worth of gain if he does not perform a 1031 Exchange.

ROBERT'S GAIN AND PROCEEDS LIVING IN CALIFORNIA

PURCHASE PRICE	$100,000
IMPROVEMENTS	$50,000
BASIS	**$150,000**
SALES PRICE	$1,000,000
COSTS OF SALE	$70,000
LOAN PAYOFF	$500,000
PROCEEDS	**$430,000**
SALES PRICE	$1,000,000
COSTS OF SALE	$70,000
BASIS	$150,000
GAIN	**$780,000**
CAPITAL GAINS TAX DUE WITH NO 1031 EXCHANGE (40%)	**$312,000**
CASH REMAINING AFTER TAXES	**$118,000**

[1]

_____

[1] This table is for the purpose of illustration only and may not represent any specific investor's results.

Depending on the state in which Robert lives and other factors, his capital gains tax will be 15–40 percent of his gain. Remember the chart from Chapter 1 showing the factors contributing to capital gains tax? If poor Robert lives in California, his capital gains tax could be as much as $312,000, which only leaves him $118,000 cash out of the sale of his million dollar investment property. Robert's poor cash out situation is because he had a $500,000 loan on the property, which he added at some time over his years of ownership. As you can see, capital gains tax can take a very big bite out of how much money is left in his pocket after the sale. In some cases, it can even mean Robert walks away with nothing. In extreme circumstances with an even larger loan on the property, Robert would need to find money from elsewhere in his estate to pay the property taxes due.

In the example above, you can see that it is vital not to over-encumber your property. In the real world, owing $500,000 against a $1 million property is very reasonable, but in Robert's case, upon sale he might wonder what happened to the other $500,000. At the time that Robert took the $500,000 cash out refinance of his property, he likely made good use of those funds. Now, however, upon sale, he's finally paying for that benefit. A 1031 Exchange means you don't pay capital gains tax when you close on your sale; you can reinvest the entire proceeds. You can also take cash from the close and not put it through the 1031

Exchange process. The amount of cash you take is called "boot." You'll pay capital gains tax on any money you "touch," but the remainder can go through the 1031 Exchange process to avoid paying capital gains taxes at the close.

The majority of DSTs come prepackaged with a loan. The individual investor does not have to go through a loan approval process; the loan is part of the investment itself. The loan is secured by the property and the Sponsor guarantees it. That means, for example, an investor can buy a property with a 50 percent loan-to-value, and with a cash investment of $100,000, the investor will own $200,000 worth of property. If the investor was coming out of a relinquished property where they had no loan, they just bought twice as much property as they actually needed to in order to successfully complete a full 1031 Exchange. That can be a win for many investors, and I'll explain why in a moment.

If the investor had a loan against their former property, and if they purchased a DST with a sufficient loan packaged with it to make an even exchange, the loan on the DST means they've satisfied the criteria for 1031 Exchange and do not have to pay capital gains tax at the close of sale. The entire amount cash out of their relinquished property can be invested. Instead of winding up with little in their pockets, as in Robert's case, they take all the cash out of the sale and invest it in available properties that match their loan needs.

Investors who sell a property that was debt free and purchase replacement property through a 1031 Exchange that has debt on it enjoy several advantages as a result of the new loan. Say for example, an investor buys a replacement property with a 50 percent loan-to-value. Assume she had no loan on her relinquished property. First, by buying twice as much property as she sold, she will have a new depreciation schedule to protect her monthly income from taxes. Second, in owning twice as much property as she sold, she will enjoy twice as much potential appreciation upon sale. Third, if the Sponsor borrows at an interest rate lower than the projected cash flow for the property, the difference between the cash flow and the interest paid on the loan is extra income for the investor. Lastly, the loans are "non-recourse," meaning the investor isn't responsible for paying them back if there is a default. The property is security against the loan, and only the Sponsor is responsible for it. Utilizing debt in real estate investing always increases risk; therefore it's very important to be mindful the size of the loan. In offerings available today, loans typically range in scale from roughly 45–60 percent loan-to-value.

Back in the 2000s, the glory days of TICs, it was common to see loans at 65–80 percent of the value of the property. Some of those properties were lost because when property values crashed in the Great Recession, the properties were worth less than the loans due on them. It is very important that we are mindful of loan size and keep it as low as possible to control risk. There are also a handful of offerings each year that have no loans, which will suit investors who aren't interested in the advantages loans provide.

Depreciation

Depreciation is another thick concept, but it's worth spending a few minutes to understand it. Depreciation, as an income tax deduction, represents the cost of replacing items that wear out. For real estate, the improvements can be depreciated. Looking at any property, a certain amount of its value is in the land, which we cannot depreciate, because land is not something that will need to be replaced (except for properties having mineral rights where depletion is a factor). The balance is the buildings and improvements that represent a potential income tax deduction.

The IRS presumes that residential property improvements (including multifamily apartment and student housing) will last 30 years, and other commercial property improvements will last 40 years. Using an example of a $5,000,000 residential property, of which $1,000,000 represents land, the remaining $4,000,000 is considered "improvements to the land", and may be divided by 30 years, giving the owner a tax deduction of $133,333 every year for 30 years. If the property was office or retail, for example, the depreciation would last 40 years and result in $100,000 in annual deductions. Depreciation is used on your tax return, Schedule E, as an expense, and is itemized in just the same way as loan interest paid, insurance or repairs. It's a straight deduction from your income on the property.

This is another important consideration when selecting the type of property in which you will invest. I advise my clients to focus on potential after-tax cash flow in their evaluation of which properties to buy, and not on gross cash flow. A retail property may have a 6.5 percent projected pre-tax net cash flow, and a multifamily apartment just 6.0 percent. However, I often find that multifamily apartment and student housing offerings can provide a higher after tax cash flow than retail properties as a result of their shorter depreciation schedule. See the illustration below.

In the illustration on the next page, the multifamily apartment property shows a 5.77 percent cash on cash (cash flow) after tax, and the retail property shows only a 5.63 percent cash on cash after tax. You can see how important depreciation becomes. The more you can depreciate each year, the lower your tax bill. A lower tax bill translates directly into dollars into your pocket. Maximizing depreciation is an important tax component of DSTs. It's one of the reasons that I favor multifamily apartment and student housing offerings.

DEPRECIATION IN RESIDENTIAL PROPERTY VS. ALL OTHER

ASSUMPTIONS	MULTIFAMILY PROPERTY	RETAIL PROPERTY
PROPERTY VALUE	$5,000,000	$5,000,000
PERCENT LAND	20%	20%
PERCENT IMPROVED	80%	80%
DEPRECIATION SCHEDULE	30 YEARS	40 YEARS
EQUITY	50%	50%
DEBT	50%	50%
TOTAL INCOME	$400,000	$405,000
TOTAL EXPENSE	$250,000	$242,400
NET INCOME	$150,000	$162,600
CASH ON CASH BEFORE TAXES	6.00%	6.50%

RESULTS

	MULTIFAMILY PROPERTY	RETAIL PROPERTY
ANNUAL DEPRECIATION EXPENSE (2)	$133,333	$100,000
TAXABLE INCOME (3)	$16,667	$62,600
TAX RATE	35%	35%
TAX DUE (4)	$5,833	$21,910
AFTER TAX INCOME (5)	$144,167	$140,690
CASH ON CASH AFTER TAXES (6)	5.77%	5.63%

1. Net income is Total Income - Total Expense
2. This may be considered roughly equivalent to the projected first year cash flow shown in the offering documents and is calculated (Total Income - Total Expense) / (Equity Percent X Property Value)
3. For Residential Property, Annual Depreciation is (Property Value X Improvement Percentage / 30 Years. For Other Property, Annual Depreciation is (Property Value X Improvement Percentage) / 40 Years
4. Taxable Income is Income Before Depreciation - Depreciation Expense
5. Tax Due is Tax Rate X Taxable Income
6. After Tax Income is Income Before Depreciation - Tax Due
6. Cash on Cash After Taxes is After Tax Income

When executing a 1031 Exchange, your depreciation history follows you to the new transaction. If you were allowed to deduct $10,000 a year in depreciation under your old depreciation schedule for your relinquished property, this would carry forward into your new investment until that original 30 or 40 year depreciation schedule is exhausted. However, if you buy $200,000 worth of property with a $100,000 loan on it and you've paid off the loan on your old property, the new $100,000 will now have its own, new depreciation schedule. This is to your advantage.

Let's say for example you bought multifamily apartment property with a 30-year depreciation term where 80 percent of the property was improvements. You now have an additional amount of tax deduction you didn't have before, merely by buying a property with a loan on it. As you take this investment and roll it into the next investment and the next one, you can piggyback additional depreciation schedules. The cumulative effect becomes potent.

Here's a hypothetical analysis of how depreciation expense can grow over time. The details are shown in Appendix V. Here are the assumptions:

1. Buy a duplex with $500,000 down and a $500,000 loan. The amount of improvements on the property is 60 percent and the land is valued at 40 percent.

2. Sell the duplex ten years later and capture your appreciation (7 percent per year) and any pay down of loan principal.

3. Take all the proceeds and 1031 Exchange into DSTs with a 50 percent loan-to-value. The DSTs are assessed at 80 percent improvements and 20 percent land value.

4. After 7.5 years, the DSTs sell and you will capture your appreciation (2 percent per year) and any pay down of loan principal.

5. Take all the proceeds and 1031 Exchange into another group of DSTs with a 50 percent loan-to-value. The DSTs are assessed at 80 percent improvements and 20 percent land value.

6. After 7.5 years, the DSTs sell and you will capture your appreciation and any pay down of loan principal.

The results are shown below in an illustration.

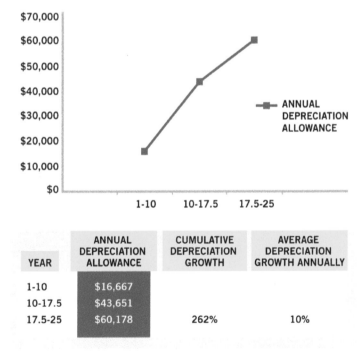

ANNUAL DEPRECIATION ALLOWANCE

YEAR	ANNUAL DEPRECIATION ALLOWANCE	CUMULATIVE DEPRECIATION GROWTH	AVERAGE DEPRECIATION GROWTH ANNUALLY
1-10	$16,667		
10-17.5	$43,651		
17.5-25	$60,178	262%	10%

I'm only presenting a 25-year example, but most investors plan to sequentially exchange until their deaths, at which point their heirs will inherit the properties at a "stepped-up basis." This is a *significant estate planning tool* to use to your benefit. The estate may experience estate tax if it's a very large estate, but the capital gains tax burden accumulated over twenty-five years of ownership disappears upon death under current tax code.

As I mentioned above, having a loan on your property increases risk. We need to be mindful of the size of the loan (loan-to-value) and be certain that we have more than ample monthly cash flow to make the loan payment each month (debt service coverage ratio). A conservative debt service coverage ratio for multifamily apartment property is 1.75 or higher. If debt service coverage ratio equals 2.0, for example, that means we have enough cash each month after expenses to make the loan payment twice over. In an effort to control risk, Sponsors will stress test their income and expense projections to determine the break-even level where net income just covers the monthly loan payment.

One more note on depreciation: the Sponsors of your DSTs will provide you with the information you need for your taxes each year. This information should be given to your tax advisor so you can secure the best tax advantage of any deductions you may be allowed.

As I mentioned earlier, I live in Silicon Valley. Residential property values here are typically assessed at 60–80 percent land value and 20–40 percent improvement value. Again, we can only depreciate the improvements, so you can see that investors in this area receive a comparatively smaller depreciation allowance on a percentage basis relative to most of the rest of the country. Here is a visual on this concept.

MULTIFAMILY ASSESSMENT VALUES

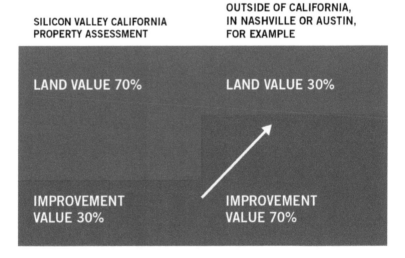

SILICON VALLEY CALIFORNIA
PROPERTY ASSESSMENT

OUTSIDE OF CALIFORNIA,
IN NASHVILLE OR AUSTIN,
FOR EXAMPLE

LAND VALUE 70%

LAND VALUE 30%

IMPROVEMENT
VALUE 30%

IMPROVEMENT
VALUE 70%

When I help my clients reinvest outside of California, we usually buy properties that are assessed at 70–80 percent improvements, the basis for depreciation, and 20–30 percent land value. For any amount of property ownership my clients invest in above the amount of their relinquished sales price, they usually will enjoy two or three times the depreciation tax shelter they did in California. That's more good news.

Congratulations on making it through this chapter! Diversification, loans, and depreciation are not for the faint of heart. But you can see how even a rudimentary understanding of current tax law and strategy will make a difference between a mediocre return and a fantastic one. Please consult with your tax advisor regarding depreciation, 1031 Exchange and other advantages the DST structure offers regarding taxes. If you need a good tax advisor for DSTs, perhaps I can help you find one.

In the next chapter, we'll talk about the experience of owning DSTs and why it's so important to choose your advisor carefully. You want to partner with someone who's a consummate expert as you continue to build your estate, increase your cash flow, and help to secure your future.

BlueRock's Clearwater DST, Clearwater, FL *This multifamily apartment property is situated equidistant from Tampa and St. Petersburg, FL and is 15 minutes away from the beautiful Gulf Beaches.*

CHAPTER 6

The Experience of Ownership: A New Lease on Life

If you own a traditional 1–4 unit rental property, and if you spend a good deal of time actively managing that property, you are probably well aware of the dreaded **Five Ts**—toilets, tenants, trash, taxes, and termites. It takes work—some properties require repairs and upgrades more than others. Managing the tenant relationship can be a strain.

Owning DSTs is a vastly different experience. No longer do the Five Ts run your life. The time that you used to devote to managing your property is now freed up for your personal life. My clients experience a broad range of emotions when they transition out of their existing investments into

DSTs, but the initial feeling is almost always the same: tremendous relief. They are liberated. They have a new lease on life. They are finally diversified. They have more time and fewer worries.

The Dynamics of Relief

The relief my clients feel is not restricted to a newfound abundance of time: they also likely enjoy increased cash flow. Less time equals more money—an equation that seems too good to be true, but it does, in fact, add up.

Assuming the investment is structured on a sound business plan driven by very active professional managers, DSTs often provide superior cash flow to anything a single investor can do. We've talked about *why* this is the case: by marshaling the significant management experience of the Sponsors, your income is increased while your expenses are reduced. Management expertise is one of the primary benefits of ownership, and a huge reason investing in DSTs can offer immediate relief with significant rewards down the line.

In place of the Five Ts come monthly or quarterly written reports from the Sponsor. These reports keep you, the investor, updated on the progress of the property relative to the business plan. You can also contact the investor relations department or any employee of the Sponsor to ask questions or gather additional information. Conference calls are often held quarterly regarding the property performance and status; if there is an issue or problem at the property, the Sponsor will usually hold a special conference call. The Sponsor will also send an annual tax package for your CPA or tax professional to use in preparing your returns.

When you receive your first monthly direct deposit or check from the Sponsor, it's an exciting experience. The research, investigation, and legwork are over. Before long it becomes routine to see your direct deposits appear in your account. The deposits are often multiples of the cash flow you've been accustomed to receiving from the property you sold, enhancing your income, and consequently your quality of life.

Another relief point for investors is diversification. When you have all or most of your assets invested in one piece of property, or several properties in one region, an ever-present chorus of "what if" may be in your thoughts. What if there's an earthquake, hurricane, or flood? What happens when the largest employer in the area goes through a round of layoffs or moves out altogether? What if your tenant leaves and you have a major property renovation on your hands, either due to the age of the property or damage incurred by the tenant?

With DSTs, that nagging chorus of woes and worries fades to silence. You no longer have one tenant in one property in one location. You're now invested across the country, in different types of real estate, with several different DSTs. One catastrophe will not devastate your portfolio.

Yet another aspect of DSTs that offers relief is the time-frame. In the past, on average, DSTs have had a lifespan of five to seven years. Once the initial work of selecting the investments is complete, you get to relax for several years and let the professionals actively manage.

In the meantime, those managers are hard at work. In a multifamily apartment property, the first two years are usually slated for making improvements while simultaneously increasing rents. Improvements may entail remodeling the units, renovating the pool or clubhouse, or installing new patio furniture, a business center, or a dog park. As improvements are implemented, new tenants will be willing to pay higher rents. Lease renewals will be at higher rents too. The Sponsor continues to operate the property, working to increase income and reduce expenses, year after year, until it becomes advantageous to sell and move on to the next investment.

Here's an insider tip that many of my clients appreciate: you might consider buying property in a place you enjoy visiting, or close to where your children or grandchildren live. My clients who choose this route will schedule visits to their investments to coincide with a vacation or family visit, thereby crafting a trip that can be a business expense. When there are quality properties available in areas with a special connection, this can be a fun and economically advantageous side benefit to DSTs.

Four Types of Risk

No investment is 100 percent risk-free, and DSTs are no different. I've witnessed hundreds of clients experience relief, elation, excitement, and a dramatically improved lifestyle after they've exchanged their traditional investments for TICs or DSTs, but they do so with full awareness of the attendant risks. I would be doing you a disservice if I didn't offer you a thoughtful and cogent analysis of the risk factors as well.

There are many risks associated with owning real estate, and DSTs are no different. The four primary risks associated with DSTs will be discussed in detail: real estate risk, operator risk, interest rate risk, and liquidity risk. In Appendix I, you will find a comprehensive list of the risks involved in DST investing. As I mentioned in my introduction to the book, the most you can lose in a DST is the equity you used to purchase the investment. The loan on your property is non-recourse to you.

Real Estate Risk

While it is regulated and sold as a security, at its core, DSTs are real estate, and the risks inherent in any real estate investment apply. Real estate risk in this context is exactly equivalent to the real estate you presently own, including your own home. The local market can drop, the economy can decline, or a tornado can cut a swath through the town.

All of these events will affect the condition, income and expense, and eventual sales price of the property.

While no one has a crystal ball, there are ways to proactively mitigate these kinds of risks. We've discussed some useful strategies in previous chapters, including ensuring you have a well-diversified portfolio in markets that are growing. And don't underestimate the importance of spending sufficient time at the outset to ensure the property is a good investment. Is it in the middle of Tornado Alley? Sitting on a fault line? Perched precariously on the coastline where hurricanes strike regularly? If the answer to any of these questions is "yes," be certain that the property insurance protects against such catastrophes.

Operator Risk

Poor management is another common risk in all real estate. When the property is not managed at an optimal level, return is always affected. Both a Property Manager and an Asset Manager manage DSTs, and each are assigned different roles.

A quick review of how management duties are divided: the Property Manager's job is to implement the business plan, increase income and lower expenses. As a result, net operating income will increase over time. The Asset Manager watches the property as if he owned it himself, managing the Property Manager with the same goal of increasing net operating income as much as possible, which increases your cash flow and appreciation potential. The Asset Manager also watches the market for sales opportunities and decides when it's time to sell, reports to investors periodically, and is responsible for keeping the investors abreast of what's going on with the property and answering any questions.

Operator risk spikes if the Property Manager or Asset Manager isn't doing a good job, or—worst-case scenario—if there is fraud involved. But again, you do have some control over this potential risk. While you can't account for the idiosyncrasies of human behavior, you *can* make a point of only working with highly experienced Sponsors who have excellent track records and sterling reputations. Have candid conversations with the people who will be in charge of your investment, and determine for yourself whether they have the character and experience to make sound judgments in your best interest.

Interest Rate Risk

We do everything humanly possible to control real estate and operator risk through our due diligence. Interest rate risk is a little different. This type of risk varies, depending on the type of DST you select. It's easiest to demonstrate in the retail space.

One of the attractive elements of Triple Net retail investments is having long-term leases in place with major tenants. Turnover will be low, and the corporation often guarantees the lease payments. In such a long lease, the lease payments don't increase frequently, perhaps every five years—and they only increase a small amount. The terms of your lease dictate yield and cash flow.

If your retail property has a ten-year lease with a yield of 5 percent, and five years from now all other comparable properties on the marketplace have leases in place that allow for a yield of 7 percent or 8 percent, you've lost potential income. The same long-term fixed lease that gives you security and keeps the yield from shifting downward with the market also doesn't allow the yield to shift upward. It's entirely possible that you won't keep up with inflation.

This risk is most often seen in retail and office properties, the ones that lend themselves to longer-term leases. One of the ways to control this risk is to invest in multifamily apartment DSTs or smaller retail units, because rents can be raised or lowered with the market. Of course, if the local marketplace doesn't allow raising rents, you will remain at the same yield level and length of lease, but you have much more opportunity to make adjustments with shorter-term leases.

Liquidity Risk

DSTs are illiquid investments. When you consider that you likely have held your current investment real estate for more than seven years, an anticipated hold period for DSTs of five to seven years on average doesn't seem so long. The hold period could be shorter or longer, depending on market conditions. There is currently no secondary market for DST ownership shares. The industry has no "multiple listing service" as in traditional fee simple real estate ownership. It is possible to sell your shares back to the Sponsor or to another investor in the DST. However, it is likely the shares would sell at a discount, not a premium, to the purchase price you originally paid. I advise my investors that this is a long-term investment, just like their relinquished property in their 1031 Exchange.

Navigating real estate risk, operator risk, interest rate risk and liquidity risk can be tricky, but less so when you're armed with the appropriate experience and expertise. It's essential to have an experienced advisor guide you through the process. With a proper understanding of all the variables at play, these risks can be greatly reduced.

Who You Work With Matters

DSTs are not a garden-variety investment. They are complicated investments with many moving parts. The underlying real estate is fundamentally important. Not all investments, even in this space, are created equal. Neither are the people who offer them to you for your consideration.

Just because a registered representative has the correct securities registrations and *can* sell this type of investment doesn't mean they have the depth of real estate experience and wisdom to be able to guide you toward the most advantageous position.

Personally vetting the Sponsors and physically visiting the properties can make a crucial difference. A highly skilled registered representative doesn't simply rely on their broker/dealer to perform due diligence: the broker/dealer is simply the initial line of screening. A qualified advisor will conduct a second, thorough review of the investments on your behalf. You'll know your advisor takes this level of care if they're on the road a good portion of the time. Ask your advisor if they see the properties they show you. Ask to see the pictures they took on their tour. Advisors taking a hands-on approach to investing will want to see most, if not all, of the properties in which they place their clients. It's a lot of extra work and takes a lot of time, but the difference in outcome for you can be substantial.

I know investors who have worked with registered representatives that send them stacks of different DST offering packages from their company approved property list, and then and ask the client to "pick one." But the quality of a real estate investment cannot be determined from the written offering materials alone. It has to be seen and experienced. A good advisor knows this. He or she will insist you get to know the Sponsor, the property, and how the investment is structured for your own peace of mind. Nothing will substitute for having the feedback about a property from an advisor who has actually seen it.

CHAPTER 7

Sequential Savings:
Say Goodbye to Capital Gains

DSTs are the gifts that keep on giving. We have touched on many of the benefits investors enjoy, from diversified portfolios to liberation from the tyranny of the Five Ts. These are the personal benefits. Then, of course, there are the attractive financial benefits.

Most traditional rental properties managed by individuals do not generate maximum cash flow. It's not uncommon for me to run a cash flow analysis (see example below) for a client's investment and discover that a property with a fair market value of over $1 million with no loan only provides the owners with $20,000 in income—a 2 percent return.

Projected annual cash flow for DSTs, however, is currently in the 5-6.75 percent range after all expenses. Moreover, most of the Sponsors I choose to work with have achieved *9 percent or higher* historical average annual internal rate of return on properties they've purchased, operated and sold for their investors, as you saw in Chapter 1. Internal rate of return includes appreciation and pay down of loan principal in addition to cash flow and is calculated when a property is sold.

Here's another financial benefit of DSTs: many investors have exhausted the depreciation schedule on the property they currently own. The tax shelter provided by that depreciation has ended, and as a result, the investor's after-tax rate of return suffers. A switch from residential one-to-four unit investments to DSTs may allow for new depreciation, once again reactivating the tax benefits of real property ownership. Investing in a property with a loan can increase your after-tax benefit even more, as I outlined in Chapter 5.

Taxes are of the utmost importance, but so far we've only given them a cursory nod. In Chapter 2 we discussed the many attractive benefits of 1031 Exchange and how investing in DSTs defers capital gains tax. But it gets even better. In this chapter, we'll take it a step further. With *sequential* 1031 Exchanges, your capital gains tax can disappear forever.

Sequential 1031 Exchanges "turbo charge" the financial benefit by harnessing the power of current tax law to completely wipe out capital gains tax. As you might imagine, this is an invaluable tool to have in your toolkit. No capital gains tax means you get to keep a good deal more of your profit instead of paying taxes to Uncle Sam.

Sequential 1031 Exchanges: A Case Study

The average investment term of a DST has been five to seven years in the past. The Sponsor makes the decision to sell when the market for a sale is advantageous. When the property is sold, the investor has a decision to make. The proceeds of the sale can be cashed out, the capital gains tax paid, and the net cash-out used in any manner the investor wishes. Or the proceeds can be reinvested by performing another 1031 Exchange. The replacement properties purchased can be DSTs or any other real estate considered like-kind by the IRS.

When an investor chooses to move their proceeds into another 1031 Exchange, all of the benefits of the original exchange are compounded. The old capital gains tax that was deferred in the original exchange remains deferred, and the potential tax on the capital gains from the sale of the DST is also deferred.

To illustrate the compounding power of sequential 1031 Exchanges, let's go back to look at Robert's situation mentioned in Chapter 5. I showed how using loans can add to your depreciation tax shelter. The actual calculations I used are shown in Appendix V and are greatly simplified for illustration purposes, and there's no assurance that investors will achieve similar results.

Robert bought a duplex in 2005 for $1,000,000 with $500,000 cash and a $500,000 loan. Today the duplex is worth about $1,950,000, and Robert decides he's ready to sell. He is sixty now, on the cusp of retirement, and ready to bid the Five Ts goodbye.

SEQUENTIAL EXCHANGES: ROBERT'S REAL ESTATE PORTFOLIO OVER 25 YEARS

YEAR PURCHASED	2005	2015	2022
PROPERTY	DUPLEX	DST1	DST2
EQUITY INVESTED	$500,000	$1,420,678	$1,958,043
PURCHASE PRICE	$1,000,000	$2,841,356	$3,916,086
SALES PRICE	$1,967,150	$3,296,301	$4,543,113
YEAR SOLD	2015	2022	2030
TAXABLE GAIN	$420,678	$1,284,396	$1,911,423
DEFERRED TAXES	$147,237	$449,539	$668,998
PROCEEDS FROM SALE	$1,420,678	$1,958,043	$2,686,240

Robert sells the duplex for $1,967,150 and has $1,420,678 in proceeds after the costs of sale. Using a 1031 Exchange, Robert avoids approximately $147,000 in capital gains tax using a 35 percent total capital gains tax rate. He invests his proceeds into one DST, ignoring my advice to purchase three or four and diversify for added safety. The new DST he buys has a 50 percent loan-to-value ratio, allowing him to purchase $2,841,356 in property value.

After 7.5 years, Robert's DST investment sells, and the sales price is $3,296,301. He invested $1,420,678 equity in the properties and receives $1,958,043 after the sale. We calculate his gain by adding his original basis in the duplex, $1,000,000, to the amount of additional property he bought when he invested in the DST, $1,011,095 (again, oversimplified). His new basis is $2,011,095. His total capital gain now is $1,284,396. If he decides to take the proceeds and cash out, his capital gains tax will be approximately $450,000. Instead, Robert reinvests all the proceeds into another DST and again ignores my advice to buy four to six DSTs and diversify his holdings. The new DST has a 50 percent loan-to-value ratio, so he now owns $3,916,086 worth of property in his new DST. He is now almost sixty-eight years old.

Robert held the DST and received cash flow and tax benefits over his years of ownership. Sadly, just before Robert's last DST sold, he passed away at the age of seventy-five, leaving his property to his daughter. The property sold a few months later for a little above $4,500,000. Robert had more than quadrupled his original investment of $500,000 in the duplex twenty-five years ago. His daughter inherited the $2,686,240 proceeds from the sale at a "stepped up basis" and owed no capital gain taxes on the sale (under current tax guidelines). Robert accumulated a $1.9 million gain over his twenty-five years of real estate ownership, and had he lived, he would have paid $668,998 in capital gains taxes upon the sale if he'd cashed out. Robert knew about 1031 Exchange and used it to help get more income every year from his investments and provide his daughter with a sizable inheritance. A stunning $668,998 that would have been paid to the government in capital gains tax remained in his estate, earning cash flow and appreciating in value over time.

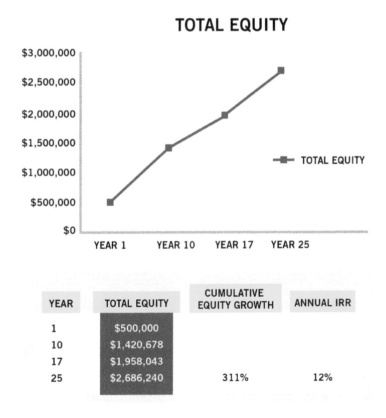

TOTAL EQUITY

YEAR	TOTAL EQUITY	CUMULATIVE EQUITY GROWTH	ANNUAL IRR
1	$500,000		
10	$1,420,678		
17	$1,958,043		
25	$2,686,240	311%	12%

As his portfolio grew, Robert's rate of return remained roughly constant. But as the value of his investment portfolio grew, so did his cash flow and his overall profit from appreciation. He lived a progressively better lifestyle as he aged, in sharp contrast to the millions of Americans who, at serious risk of outlasting their retirement funds, will be forced to downsize every aspect of their lives.

Step-Up in Cost Basis

According to current tax law, all the capital gains taxes deferred along the way are entitled to the step-up in cost basis upon death. This rule means the heirs will receive the portfolio with the same value as it held on the date of death. The substantial accumulated capital gains tax deferred over the years vanishes, and the family or charity inherits the entire portfolio at its current market value. *No capital gains taxes are due—EVER!* The taxes that would have been paid remain in the estate. The equity grows over time, and annual cash flow increases, even if the rate of return is constant.

I cannot overstate the power and importance of that concept. I've had calls from people who had paid hundreds of thousands of dollars in capital gains tax. It was hard-earned money that had the potential to change their lives, or their children's or grandchildren's lives. To be able to sidestep capital gains tax completely is a wonderful opportunity to transfer wealth between generations, sometimes shaving

DOES YOUR STATE HAVE AN ESTATE OR INHERITANCE TAX?

STATE HAS AN ESTATE TAX

CT	DE	DC	HI	IL	MA	ME
$2M	$5.43M	$1M	$5.43M	$4M	$1M	$2M
7.2%-12%	0.8%-16%	0.8%-16%	0.8%-16%	0.8%-16%	0.8%-16%	8%-12%

MN	NY	OR	RI	TN	WA
$1.4M	$3.125M	$1M	$1.5M	$5M	$2.054M
9%-16%	3.06%-16%	0.8%-16%	0.8%-16%	5.5%-9.5%	10%-20%

STATE HAS AN INHERITANCE TAX

IA	KY	NE	PA
0%-15%	0%-16%	1%-18%	0%-15%

STATE HAS BOTH

MD	NJ
$1.5M	$2M
16%	7.2%-12%

NOTE: Exemption amounts are shown for state estate taxes only. Inheritance taxes are levied on the posthumous transfer of assets based on the relationship to the decendent; different rates and exemptions apply depending on the relationship.

SOURCE: U.S. Census Bureau; state statutes; Family Business Coalition

Tax rates are subject to change. Please consult with your tax advisor to determine your individual circumstances.

millions of dollars off the bill. Generally when inheritance occurs in DSTs, the heirs will leave the investments in place until the properties sell in their natural life cycle. They can then cash out or continue on their path of sequential 1031 Exchanges to continue to defer their own capital gains taxes.

Note that the estate taxes may still be due depending on tax law as of the date of death and size of the estate. Currently, the exemption amount is set at $11.2 million with a top federal tax rate of 40 percent. Any estate valued at less than $11.2 million will not incur estate tax at a federal level. At the state level, estate taxes range from zero to twenty percent on estates as low as $675,000 or more in value.

Estate Planning

While estate planning sits outside the purview of this book, it bears a mention in this chapter. I have seen far too many families without the necessary plan in place. Any candidate for DSTs is by definition an accredited investor under the SEC guidelines, which means they have significant income and/or assets. To ignore necessary estate planning would be shortsighted. The benefits of proper estate planning are:

- Avoidance of probate, a lengthy and expensive court process that invites challenges and gives the court control over your entire estate
- Planning for disability and medical wishes

- Minimization of taxes on the nest egg you have spent a lifetime accumulating
- Allowing your assets to be immediately accessible to continue to manage your obligations after death, including providing for your funeral
- Making your passing much easier on your family and the people you love.

Take a day to meet with an estate attorney and make sure your family will not be simultaneously grieving you while also suffering the burden of having to manage a haphazardly planned estate. The cost for a living trust can be as little as $2,500 and require a day's total time for you. Measure that against your opportunity cost in time and money without a living trust, and your heirs' potential frustration during this difficult time.

The Beauty of Sequential Savings

The gift of sequential 1031 Exchanges is that your money keeps making you more money—all you have to do is reinvest it. Sequential 1031 Exchanges can provide a significant increase in the size of the original investment over a period of years while simultaneously avoiding capital gains (and potential estate) taxes.

Consequently, you'll enjoy a steady stream of cash flow that continues to increase. Like Robert, you'll live better and better as you get older.

CHAPTER 8

Why Doesn't My Realtor Know About This?

When considering DSTs, some people wonder why their Realtor hasn't presented them as an option. After all, this is a real estate offering; it concerns real property. Why don't you hear about it first from your trusted real estate agent?

While Realtors are in the business of buying and selling property, syndicated real estate investing falls outside of their expertise and licensing. It's related but different. It's like expecting your car mechanic to work on your airplane. Certain skill sets may overlap, but you'd be foolish to drive your airplane into the car shop expecting a full repair.

The vast majority of Realtors successfully assist their clients in buying and selling residential property, defined as 1–4 units. Multifamily apartment DSTs are done on a much larger scale, generally with a minimum of two hundred units. Also, syndicated real estate is offered as a security, which requires industry participants to be properly licensed and to have securities registrations. As a result, few Realtors are aware of syndicated real estate as an investment option, and even fewer know the nuances and subtleties of the industry.

DSTs are more likely to cross the path of a commercial real estate agent than the agent who sold you your house. Commercial real estate agents tend to be more investment-oriented, and they may come from a business background where they were exposed to financial analysis. However, commercial real estate agents are also not licensed securities representatives or investment advisors and do not have access to the DST market.

Realtor Outreach

Although DSTs aren't within Realtors' training or licensing, I've known many Realtors eager for more knowledge about this type of investment. They want to be fully informed about investment options for their clients and themselves. I routinely educate interested Realtors on the ins and outs of DSTs. I also hold seminars for leading agents who want to offer their clients a full stable of real estate options. They know that the partnership between a residential or commercial real estate agent and an investment advisor who specializes in real estate can be very strong. Each professional brings his or her body of knowledge and experience to the table, and by working as a team, we can create a dynamic result for the client.

Realtors often come into contact with the type of investors described in this book; people tired of hands-on management who are seeking higher cash flow to help fund current or future retirement. But Realtors don't always know of a better alternative. They, like the investors themselves, are under the impression that the capital gains taxes will be exorbitant if their clients sell their current property. Also, many Realtors are aware of 1031 Exchanges, but have never heard of DSTs.

When Realtors become exposed to the mechanics and structuring of a 1031 Exchange, they can urge their clients to explore the available tax benefits of selling their investment property. On a macro level, when Realtors understand the concepts in this book, they can present a very attractive investment option to their clients. At that point, the client has compelling reasons to consider selling current properties instead of keeping rental units that no longer satisfy his or her personal and financial needs.

Real Estate vs. Security

We talked a bit about how DSTs are essentially real estate packaged as a security. There is an important distinction, one that will help you see why a securities license is required for all advisors in my field.

In 1946, in *SEC vs. W.J. Howey Co.*, The Supreme Court identified the characteristics of an investment contract for the purposes of the Securities Act of 1933. This is called the *Howey Test*. They are:

- Investment of money due to
- An expectation of profits arising from
- A common enterprise
- Which depends solely on the efforts of a promoter or third party.

Any time you bring unrelated people together to raise funds for an investment meeting these criteria, you're offering a security (with few exceptions), and the SEC has guidelines in place to protect consumers. While the SEC does not require the advisor to be knowledgeable in the field of real estate to sell DSTs, they do want accountability and recourse for fraud or failing to follow guidelines. It's similar to the practice of law. The law requires a licensed attorney who has proven competency via education and testing to comply with ethical regulations, and is accountable to a regulating entity like the state bar.

Similarly, the SEC has certain standards that must be met by representatives who want to sell securities. Think of this as a protective and precautionary measure, one that will help you sort the wheat from the chaff when it comes to selecting a competent advisor. Back in the mid-2000s, a handful of firms offered TICs as "real estate" without obtaining securities education and licenses or providing the required disclosures to their potential investors. The SEC stepped in and put a stop to it. In this way, the SEC offers a valuable service: they require that specific, exhaustive disclosures are provided to clients regarding each individual DST offering. Without such requirements, consumers could be harmed.

The Hybrid

The key, as with many things, is to strike a healthy balance. You want to find an advisor who's well versed in both real estate and securities. An advisor with that background will likely have a real estate broker's license, and may also be a certified commercial investment member (CCIM). These advisors are constantly expanding their knowledge in the field, both formally and informally. They are hungry to keep learning, because the more they know, the more they can help their clients.

Advisors without this level of expertise will likely only have securities licenses and be better versed in the stock market, mutual funds, retirement accounts, or annuities than in commercial real estate and DSTs. Some advisors view DSTs as a sideline to their main business; others, like me, devote all their professional energy to DSTs.

My personal recommendation to you is this: find someone who lives and breathes DSTs and who is also a real estate broker. When you're facing cancer, you don't want just any doctor; you want an oncologist, ideally the best one you can find. As much as you may like your GP or internist, she's not the person you should see for treatment, and ultimately she's not the one who could save your life.

The same principle holds true for DSTs. Your local real estate agent is a fantastic resource, especially if she can assist you in the sale of your existing property for the highest possible price. And if she's aware of DSTs as an investment option, she might be able to refer you to a registered representative or investment advisor who specializes in DSTs. She cannot guide you regarding DSTs.

No slight against her—she may very well be curious to learn more. If she hasn't recommended that you learn more about this type of investment, it's likely because she's unaware of this alternative. Once DSTs are brought to her attention, and she understands the tremendous potential for you and your portfolio, she'll be in a much better position to work closely with the expert investment advisor you choose. She may even refer an advisor to you.

CHAPTER 9

From Property to Prosperity

B y now you may be feeling cautiously hopeful. You're thinking, "Well, it *sounds* good, Leslie—at least on paper. But it's all in theory, not in practice. What does investing in DSTs actually look like? How does it work? How do I get started? What impact will these investments have on my real-life portfolio?"

Every investor is different, of course, but there *are* certain steps that everyone must take, a certain path I chart with each client I work with. As someone who has guided hundreds of clients into these investments, I have a tried-and-true process for getting clients out from under their old properties and reinvested in DSTs, and hundreds of cases to prove it. I'd like to share a few of those with you now.

In this chapter, I will profile three hypothetical cases as they move from owning individual property to DSTs. I'll take you through their journeys step by step, starting with their original situation and how they found their way to me. You'll get a peek at my process: where I start with my clients and what happens next. As we meet each of the investors, you will find areas of commonality, places where their stories may overlap with your own.

The first client, Anne, owned a fourplex. She had a friend who invested with me, and one day Anne was complaining to this friend about how tired she was of the day-to-day grind of managing the fourplex. The friend suggested she talk to me about other options.

The second client, Bill, owned a $3 million office building downtown. At a networking meeting, Bill overheard other investors discussing their DSTs. He was intrigued, got a referral from one of the investors, and contacted me.

The third client is actually a couple, Carol and Hank. They owned four single-family properties, purchased over the years as their family moved from house to house. Each time they bought a new house, they kept the old one and used it as a rental. Nearing retirement and dissatisfied with the cash flow they were receiving, especially as they anticipated dipping into their nest egg for retirement income, Carol and Hank found me online through a Google search that led them to LinkedIn (www.linkedin.com/in/lesliepappas) and then to my site, www.ArcherInvestors.com.

Getting Started

The first step for each client was a discussion with me on the phone. This call is a discovery session for both the client and me. The client gets an introduction to 1031 Exchange and syndicated investing in DSTs, and I preliminarily determine the client's accredited investor status, current situation, and potential interest in investing. All three clients had little to no knowledge about DSTs; two were aware of 1031 Exchange and its benefits. After the first call, usually 30–60 minutes in length, all three clients had a firm grasp on the investment process, and the benefits and risks of DSTs. I also routinely present Triple Net investing as a possible replacement property strategy, as I am a licensed real estate broker in several states.

As you might expect, each client had concerns. This is only natural when you're looking at investing a sizable chunk of your net worth. Anne's main concern was hands-on ownership. She was accustomed to doing everything herself on her fourplex, and the few times she had tried to hire a Property Manager, her return had been reduced significantly and the tenants complained. It was hard for her to see how anyone else would put as much time, effort, and thought into managing her property as she had.

Bill's initial concerns centered on the tax consequences of a sale. He had invested significant capital in his office building and needed to be sure that he would not lose a large portion of the gain to pay taxes if he sold. The idea of performing a 1031 Exchange really appealed to him.

Carol and Hank were afraid of the expense associated with selling their single-family properties and purchasing new properties. They had a difficult time understanding how they could sell a property, even at the height of the local market, and invest in anything better.

Each client came to our phone calls with an open mind, even though they were not familiar with this type of investment. They knew someone must own all the apartment complexes, shopping centers, and office buildings around the country, but it was hard for them to imagine *they* could be among those people. With the exception of Bill and his small office building, they had never thought about what it might be like to own such large properties.

We devoted a good amount of time to education, talking on the phone, on Skype, and in person as I explained DSTs in detail to all three clients. After this initial period, each of the clients engaged in his or her discovery process to further investigate 1031 Exchange and DSTs. Like I do with all my clients, I offered to take them to Los Angeles for a day and introduce them to some of the Sponsors I work with and learn about their current offerings, histories, strategies, track records, etc.

Anne took me up on the offer. We went together to the Los Angeles area and met with three Sponsors. Four other clients joined us there. She asked detailed questions about how Sponsors choose and manage properties, and familiarized herself with the properties each Sponsor currently had available for investment. She became convinced that the Sponsors knew much more than she did about acquiring, managing and disposing of investment properties. They were impressive professionals with superb track records and backgrounds. Anne was excited that she had learned so much about DSTs, met the three Sponsors, and learned about the industry and specific properties available at that time.

Due to his busy schedule, Bill opted not to take the day trip to Los Angeles. I arranged 30-minute webinars with three key Sponsors, and Bill and I attended them together at his convenience. He reviewed some past and current offerings and looked through the PPMs (private placement memoranda) for each. In reviewing these materials and gauging the education and experience of the principals, their staff, and me, he felt confident he was in good hands.

Carol and Hank also took the day trip with me to Los Angeles and met the Sponsors in person. They went one step further and visited a property near their home that was managed by a Sponsor with whom they were interested in investing. Carol and Hank enjoyed touring the property and asking the Property Manager questions. Reviewing its accompanying PPM allowed them to feel confident in the authenticity of DSTs. They decided these investments were definitely suitable for their portfolio, and probably a far superior investment to the single-family houses that had been running them ragged all these years.

Once each of the clients became comfortable with 1031 Exchange, DSTs, the Sponsors' abilities, and me, they were ready to list their current investment properties for sale.

I should note here that I don't always get to meet clients before they decide to sell their properties and invest with me. Often a client will contact me when their property is on the market, or even already sold, to begin the learning process. But I love working with clients who haven't yet decided to sell because I get to walk them through every step of the process—just like I'm doing with you right now.

Listing the Property

Anne listed her fourplex, Bill listed his office building, and Carol and Hank began by listing one of their four single-family residences. Anne and Bill had real estate agents they felt comfortable with, and I referred Carol and Hank to a leading agent in their area. All three of the clients worked with their real estate agents to maximize the value of the property without incurring large costs and/or undertaking significant renovations. Anne and Bill did only exterior curb appeal work because their properties would be sold to investors. Carol and Hank, on the other hand, worked on the interior as well, because their single-family home would likely be sold to a family.

If Carol and Hank had decided to sell more than one of their properties, every property would have been a separate listing and 1031 Exchange. This is why starting with one can be a good way to "test the waters." Often clients with multiple properties sell one or two properties, experience ownership of DSTs for a period of time, and then list their other properties. This is a great way for new clients to get their feet wet.

My clients kept me in the loop during the property preparation, listing, and sales process. Timelines are crucial in this industry, especially when it's time to execute a valid 1031 Exchange. If you fail to meet the deadlines, you will put the entire exchange at risk. That means you would owe capital gains taxes. In the above transactions, all parties understood that we would begin to review available offerings as soon as they had buyers in contract and their escrows were opened.

Eventually, all three clients found buyers. Escrow opened, and they each gave me a call to be sure I was in the loop.

I then contacted their escrow officer to set up their 1031 Exchange. I asked the escrow officers to send me the "seller's estimated proceeds," a preliminary calculation of all the expenses of sale, an estimate of loans on the property, and finally, the estimated proceeds. At this time, my clients and I also began the process of reviewing available offerings for their consideration.

Set the 1031 Parameters

Now that each of the three clients was in a solid escrow, there were some determinations to be made. For each client, the first determination was the amount of the loans against the relinquished property. A valid 1031 Exchange requires the investor to buy replacement property that has equal or greater value than the relinquished property being sold (minus some selling expenses). That includes the debt on the relinquished property.

By determining the amount of the loan(s) on the relinquished property, I was able to narrow the field of potential DSTs that would provide my clients with an even exchange. Each offering has a specific loan-to-value, and in each case, my clients wanted to purchase at least as much property as they sold. The seller's estimated-proceeds statement from the escrow company helped with this, but these statements never include all the final numbers we eventually need. I always also get a final statement from the escrow officer when the property closes, so I'm working from the exact numbers needed to execute an even exchange.

Each client also had to make a decision about how much of the proceeds they wanted to move into DSTs, and how much cash, if any, they wanted to take out of the proceeds (boot). Investors can do a partial exchange by allocating some of the proceeds towards a 1031 Exchange and the balance towards anything else they might desire, like a vacation or improvements on their own residence. As we've discussed, capital gains tax is due on any boot taken. Anne and Bill decided to move all of the proceeds into DSTs; Carol and Hank took a $100,000 boot as an emergency fund for their retirement.

The initial decision of how much money to take out of the sale is not a final decision, but it's good practice to get a sense of it as early in the process as possible. As soon as we determine the ballpark amount to be invested, including any loan requirements, I can identify specific properties that match the client's needs.

Setting Up the 1031 Exchange

To comply with the specific rules and regulations surrounding 1031 Exchanges, the exchange is set up soon after escrow opens on the relinquished property. Selection of a Qualified Intermediary is not a place to pinch pennies. The QI needs to be very knowledgeable about the specifics of 1031 Exchange, have a long track record of success, and be bonded. This is important because failure to properly execute the 1031 Exchange can cause the exchange to "be blown," at which point capital gains tax will be due.

I've worked with Ron Ricard at Investment Property Exchange (IPX1031.com) for over sixteen years, and never once has he failed to provide my clients with exceptional service and seasoned advice. (I cannot help giving him a plug, as he and his firm are terrific.) IPX is a national, bonded firm. I draw no benefit from recommending him to you, other than to see you succeed. Certainly research the field. There are many exchange companies to choose from, and they need not be located in your area to help execute your exchange. You will not need to visit their offices to conduct the 1031 Exchange.

My client or I will notify the QI that escrow has been opened, and connect the QI with the escrow officer who is managing the sale of the property. The earlier the paperwork can be put in place, the better. Scrambling to make a 1031 Exchange deadline is not fun for anyone and leaves room for error. It is essential to begin the process with the QI while still in escrow. If we don't, there won't be an exchange. This makes the process move smoothly and quickly.

The boot (cash out) can be paid directly to the client out of escrow, and the money for investment through 1031

Exchange will be wired directly to the QI from the relinquished property escrow account. The funds must move from escrow to the QI and then to the Sponsor's escrow account to avoid capital gains taxes at the close. Boot can be taken after the 1031 Exchange has begun, but deciding at a later date may mean a delay in receiving the cash. Some QIs will not release the remaining funds from the exchange account until all investments have been funded.

10–14 Days before the Close

Our initial offering discussions focus on the type of property that each client prefers, such as multifamily apartment, office, retail, or any subcategory of each. I always encourage diversification. In the case of Anne, Bill, and Carol and Hank, I educated each client about the pros and cons, the projected returns of each offering, and the potential tax shelter from depreciation. If I've already toured a property, I'll convey my thoughts and scroll through the eighty to one hundred photos I took when I visited. The clients become more thoroughly educated about the various Sponsors and the investments available to them when their escrow closes.

Often, the clients depend on my experience to determine which Sponsors are a good fit for them. Because of my many years in the business, I have insight into the Sponsors that doesn't show up in the marketing materials or PPMs. I want my clients to work with Sponsors who keep the investor's interests paramount in their decision-making process. I also prefer investments where the Sponsors' and investors' interests are closely aligned in one way or another.

Anne, Bill, Carol and Hank reviewed the offering materials for several different DST investments, and we had conference calls or webinars with the Sponsors involved. Using that education and my advice, we zeroed in on the top options for each client.

Choosing DSTs

By the time the escrow closes, my clients have usually settled on specific investments they feel are a good fit for them. Based on their discovery process and the level of trust we've established, some clients rely heavily on my recommendations. Other clients become more deeply involved in the property selection process, using me as a kind of oracle who answers questions, or as a sounding board off which to bounce their ideas. Either way is fine with me; it's really about the client's preference and comfort level.

Usually clients choose two to four properties for diversification from a list of about ten to twenty properties currently available. In our case studies, each client bought more than one DST investment, diversifying by geography and by Sponsor. Anne chose two multifamily apartment complexes. Bill selected two medical office properties and two retail offerings. Carol and Hank decided to start off with one multifamily apartment investment and one retail investment.

In every case, I want my clients to attend a webinar by the Sponsor, or at least a conference call so that they have the opportunity to learn more about the Sponsor and particular offerings in detail and have all their questions answered. I want my clients to be very comfortable with the Sponsors and investments they choose. I worked closely with each client to determine what would bring them that level of comfort, especially since it was Bill, Anne, Hank, and Carol's first foray into syndicated real estate.

At this point, a few days before the close of escrow, the 1031 Exchange has been set up, and the Sponsors and properties to invest in have likely been chosen. This timeframe is key, because although the 1031 Exchange guidelines from the IRS do not require this level of precision, any time the proceeds spend sitting at the QI and not invested in a new property is a loss of cash flow for my client.

When the relinquished property sale closes—sometimes even *before* it closes—I will begin to prepare investment documents. My clients and I complete new account paperwork and a financial statement to open their account with my broker/dealer. I use this account paperwork to complete investment reservation documents on behalf of my clients.

This relieves them of the burden of doing so themselves, as it's a lot of paperwork. My clients review everything I prepare, ensuring all documents are accurate and complete, and then sign or initial as indicated. I aim to make paperwork as easy as possible for my clients.

My broker/dealer reviews the paperwork and must approve the investment in order to move forward. The Sponsor reviews the documents and notifies me if we are missing anything. All documentation necessary to transfer the funds from the QI to the Sponsor is completed. No funds are moved from the QI to the investments without written consent from the client. At this point, the client will be in direct contact with the QI and each Sponsor's closing department to fund the investments. I continue to manage the closing process and am in the loop on all communications.

My goal is to have my clients reinvested within two weeks of the close of escrow on their relinquished property. The IRS allows for more time, but why delay? The IRS allows forty-five days from the close of the relinquished property to identify potential replacement property and 180 days from the close to purchase one or more of the identified properties. All the extra time does is create anxiety for my clients. I know that the sooner an investment decision is made, the easier the process is for the client. The outcome does not improve with the passage of time. It is much better to begin the process of identifying and selecting properties while still in escrow so that the proceeds can be reinvested as quickly as possible after the sale.

In case you were wondering, Anne, Bill, Carol and Hank are all very happy with their investments. They've moved from individually owned properties to institutional-grade portfolios, and all are experiencing the benefits of 1031 Exchange and DST investing, both personally and financially.

Hank and Carol, in particular, are pleased with their diversification. They've come a long way from their days of owning single-family properties. Not only do their real estate investments today have less risk by not being concentrated in one geography or one property type, they're generating significantly more cash flow. Initially, they were making around 1.5–2 percent cash flow; today that number has *more than tripled*, coming in at roughly 5 percent projected cash flow after taxes. "Thank God we found you, Leslie," Carol told me a few weeks ago. "We'll never invest in a single-family house again!"

The Experience of Ownership

Anne, Bill, Carol, and Hank have all moved from property to prosperity. Now, instead of answering late-night phone calls, they receive quarterly performance reports and participate in periodic conference calls as the Asset Manager and Property Manager execute the business plan for the property. They receive monthly direct deposits of their distributions into their account. A tax package is sent to them in the first quarter of each year, which is used to prepare their tax returns. Any time they have questions about the investment, they contact the investor relations department or any Sponsor employee they choose to get the information they need. I am also available to my clients throughout their ownership to help however I can.

I'm still in regular communication with all four of them. They're enjoying their experience of ownership in the present, but they've got an eye on the future, too. I encourage that sense of planning. As newly converted institutional investors, they should be considering future sequential 1031 Exchanges, because, at some point down the line, their existing properties will be sold.

Property sale has occurred in the past, on average, between five and seven years into ownership. I've seen a range in holding periods of two to twelve years in my practice. When the Sponsor believes investors have received the maximum benefit from ownership, the property will be sold. The investors do not have a "vote," but the Sponsor will prepare a communication and host a conference call to outline their thought process and discuss the reasons a sale is being considered.

In the case of conference calls, there is back-and-forth conversation, as well as a question-and-answer time. Often, the Sponsor will take a straw poll of investors. Because investing in DSTs is a financial exercise, not a labor of love, the property will be sold when it makes financial sense, to capture appreciation or exit before an anticipated change in the market. The investors will begin to make decisions about their next move. Sales of properties the size of DSTs take longer than residential one-to-four-unit investments—roughly sixty to ninety days, and sometimes longer, which provides time for the investors to determine what they will do next.

Anne, Bill, Carol, and Hank are in open dialogue about that "next move," which will come at different times for all of them. They're mulling over different options, excited about where their next investments will take them. One thing is certain: they'll definitely be investing in DSTs again, carrying on sequential 1031 Exchanges and reinvesting the proceeds into their next retail, office, or multifamily apartment property. Barring any major economic crisis in our country, I expect that is how the investments will unfold.

Their lives are better all around. Anne can't believe how tightly she was holding onto the reins of her former rental properties. Now that she's free of her management duties, she's been able to do things she never dreamed she'd be able to do—like go on a month-long backpacking tour of Europe with her partner. Bill is finally pursuing his passion for skiing full-force, and Hank and Carol are proudly growing college funds for their three grandchildren with their monthly DST investment distributions. All four of them have more money, more time, and more fun.

Not only that, but they are also telling everyone they know. Anne, Bill, Hank and Carol have been sharing with their friends and families the benefits of DSTs. I know because they've already sent two clients to me who are learning about DSTs right now.

CHAPTER 10

More Time, More Money, More Freedom

In this book, I've talked to you as an author, an advisor, and a licensed professional. I've given you an overview of DSTs and some of their most appealing features and shared stories and case studies from my personal experience. I've tried to provide a solid foundation for further inquiry and analysis, a kind of "crash course" in DSTs born of many years of experience.

Now I want to shake off all those fancy qualifications for a minute and talk to you person to person.

DSTs can seem complicated. I know this very well. But here's the secret about DSTs. *At their core are people.* It's not *what* you know; it's *who* you know that counts. And it's not just about the people you choose to work with—it's ultimately about you and what you want. Investments and money are only useful to the extent that they enhance lives. That's why I do what I do: to see the changes in my clients' lives.

Some professions are innately "helper" professions, like medicine and education. The way I see it, advisors are helpers as well. My tools aren't syringes and textbooks, but investment tools, knowledge, and experience. These are my stock-in-trade, the assets I offer my clients to help them move from what is often a good but challenging position into an *excellent* position, one that allows them more time with their families and more time to go out into the world and achieve meaningful things.

What I do provides freedom. Those who don't have freedom want it more than anything else. My brand of freedom is personal and financial, and its primary tools are 1031 Exchange and DSTs. If that tool is helpful to you, I would love nothing more than to step in and help.

Investing requires planning, particularly real estate investing. It's like a game of chess in that there are many moving pieces, and to stay on top of them, you must think several steps ahead. Too many times I have been on the phone with someone who has sold an investment property with an intention to reinvest, but were never presented with the option of a 1031 Exchange—and hence paid the capital gains tax. That is always a sad phone call for me. While DSTs and their benefits are still available, I mourn for the lost opportunity of that initial 1031 Exchange. I care about mistakes like this because my clients aren't just clients to me. They're people I want to see thrive in the world. No one should have to suffer those kinds of losses. Now that you've read this book, you'll never have to be one of those people. A little knowledge can go a long way.

Are We a Good Fit?

I speak with folks at many points in the investment lifecycle. I speak with people who are:

1. tired of owning individual investment property and the headaches it entails. They may also be deeply dissatisfied with the returns they're making and often are on the brink of a major life change, like retirement;

2. investigating the outcome of selling their individual investment property and casting about for a better alternative. This could be for themselves or for investments they are managing on behalf of a family member;

3. in the process of selling their investment property without a clear view of what they will do with the proceeds;

4. closed in their investment property sale and are in a 1031 Exchange, waiting for something attractive in which to invest;

5. closed in their investment property sale and are looking to purchase other residential 1-4 units, but are considering DSTs as a backup position because their 45 day identification time limit is imminent;

6. closed in their investment property sale and paid capital gains taxes either because they weren't aware of 1031 Exchange, DSTs or both.

I prefer to talk to people in the first five scenarios because all options remain open. We can craft a plan that maximizes all the potential benefits. The fifth scenario may lead to a frenetic scramble if the client's 1031 Exchange is within days, but it can be done. I've helped people with a window of two to three days comply with the 1031 Exchange rules and still get the benefits of investing in DSTs. Even in the sixth scenario, all is not lost. The personal and financial benefits of DSTs are still possible, even if the window for a 1031 Exchange has closed. Also, this is just one investment at one point in time. No one has to make the same mistake twice.

No matter where you are in the investment lifecycle, the time to learn more about DSTs is now. You gain nothing by waiting, and everything by starting the process of educating yourself. The time will come when you want to sell your property, and you won't be able to make as wise a decision if you aren't familiar with all options for reinvestment.

It All Starts with a Conversation

I wrote this book with a view toward educating readers on the benefits and process of 1031 Exchange and DSTs. This is admittedly a broad view. But you are a unique individual, and no one shares your exact circumstances. We all have different starting points and investment goals, and only you know if DSTs are right for you.

By reading this book, you may begin to put together a strategy for DSTs. But until you sit down with an advisor who is knowledgeable in the field, it's hard to understand the full impact. It all starts with a conversation. And it's as easy as picking up the phone.

Most people, including many professionals such as attorneys and CPAs, have not been exposed to DSTs. They are available only to accredited investors, and most accredited investors likely don't realize they're available. When talking to your CPA about the tax implications or to your attorney about the legal implications, be sure they have handled a multitude of 1031 Exchanges. Just like Realtors, some attorneys and CPAs are not intimately familiar with this portion of the tax code. I often sit down with professionals and their clients, either in person or via conference call, and discuss the pros and cons of 1031 Exchange and DSTs.

A common theme in this book is that *who you work with is important*. It doesn't have to be me, but it must—absolutely must—be somebody knowledgeable in both the securities and real estate aspects of DSTs. You want all the knowledge and the experience possible to make these crucial decisions about the interplay of tax, loans, depreciation, diversification, and property selection. These are the choices that will chart the course of your portfolio for the rest of your life. It may affect future generations in your family.

Advisors intimately involved in DSTs typically have the inside scoop. Offerings are open only for a short time, and they're often fully funded quickly. Because of this, inside information and strong professional relationships can be pivotal. Advisors whose entire practice revolves around DSTs, as does mine, often have close relationships with Sponsors; they know what's available now, but more importantly, they know what *will be available soon*. These advisors can express your interest to the Sponsor early, giving you an invaluable edge on the competition, vying for placement in a particular offering.

The Best Years of Your Life

You worked hard for your money over many decades. I don't have to tell you that. You worked hard on your investments, too, choosing the right ones for your portfolio, trying to make wise decisions when it came to real estate, maybe even doting on your rental properties like an expectant parent. You watched your portfolio grow, and you poured out endless resources of time, attention, and love to make it the best it could be.

It's time for that portfolio to do something for you.

As retirement grows nearer, your investments should be doing the heavy lifting, not you. Your time is valuable. So is your health. You only get one life—it's up to you how you live it. You get to determine how to spend the rest of your years. You owe it to yourself to make sure you investigate the possibilities that can provide more time, more money, and more freedom. You want to make those years the best they can be.

I love guiding people through the process of under-standing DSTs and the tremendous gift of DSTs. Please bear in mind that it is my responsibility, skill, and plea-sure to guide you through this process, as I have guided hundreds of other investors just like you. I have seen these investments create new opportunities, liberate investors, and change lives. I wouldn't have devoted my career to them if they didn't.

If you think DSTs might be a fit for you, please reach out. I'd love to show you what I've shown hundreds of others over the years. And if you have any concerns or questions of any kind, don't hesitate to give me a call.

I wish you all the best. May your portfolio be like your life: vibrant, full, and growing for many years to come. **Invest to Live, Don't Live to Invest!**™

Appendices

Risk in DST Investments: What You Need to Know

Now that we've outlined all the moneymaking potential of DST investments, I'd like to take a moment to explain the risks involved in these types of transactions. Remember, DST investments are only available to accredited investors.

Suitability

DST investments may not suitable for all investors.

Real Estate Risks

Real estate is subject to market cycles, just like any other type of investment. A piece of property may rise in value or it may fall. DSTs have the potential to provide great financial returns, but they're not immune to changes in the economy. Such risks include, but are not limited to, loss of principal, variations in occupancy (which may have a negative impact on cash flow), illiquidity, and changes to the value of the underlying investments.

Operator Risk

Investors must be willing to rely on the Trustee, the Asset Manager, and the Property Manager to make property-related decisions. Beneficial owners of the Trust possess limited control and rights. The Trust will be operated and managed solely by the Trustee, and beneficial owners have no right to participate in the management of the trust.

Interest Rate Risk

If you are invested in properties with very long leases and few increases in lease rates over time, there is a chance that your investment return will not keep up with interest rates in the marketplace.

Liquidity Risk

Like any other real estate, DST investments are illiquid. This property cannot be sold or exchanged for cash quickly. There is no established secondary market for the resale of ownership shares.

Fees and Expenses

There are fees associated with acquiring DSTs. Making the property available to multiple owners incurs expenses—including but not limited to brokerage fees and marketing, for example. In some cases these fees might even outweigh the benefits of tax deferral.

Conflicts

Registered Investment Advisors have a fiduciary duty to act in the best interests of their clients. However, brokers are not required to abide by such fiduciary standards and do *not* have to place a client's interests above their own.

Past Performance

Past performance doesn't ensure future performance. Property appreciation and projected income are not guaranteed. You may lose equity in this investment.

Tax Status

According to the IRS and Revenue Ruling 2004-86, 1031 exchanges completed through a DST are structured investments. This revenue procedure includes guidelines for taxpayers preparing ruling requests. They are only guidelines, however, and are not intended for audit purposes. Also, laws change, which means that different tax provisions may come into play, creating liabilities and penalties.

The Seven Deadly Sins

DST trustees are prohibited from committing any of the following actions:

1. Accept contributions to the DST after the period for soliciting investments is over.

2. Renegotiate the terms of existing loans or borrow new funds.

3. Reinvest proceeds from real property sale or acquire new real property.

4. Invest any cash to profit from market fluctuations.

5. Make any unnecessary property modifications unless required by law.

6. Renegotiate any master lease or enter into a new lease on the property.

7. Fail to distribute cash profits regularly.

Conclusion

Risks are inherent in any type of investment. Please keep these points in mind when making investment decisions. This material is not intended as legal or tax advice. Please consult with your accountant and attorney to ensure you are making the best decision for your circumstances.

Archer Investment Advisors is a branch of LightPath Capital, Inc. Securities offered through LightPath Capital, Inc. Member FINRA / SIPC. This is neither an offer to sell nor a solicitation of an offer to buy securities. The information in this book alone should not be used in making investment decisions. The Prospectus is controlling. Investors should carefully consider the investment objectives, risks, charges, and expenses associated with any investment.

APPENDIX II

Accredited Investor
Qualifications & Disclosures

It's estimated that **8.25 percent of all American house-holds—roughly 10 million households**—qualified as *accredited investors in 2013.*[1] Accredited investors have access to a broad array of investment options that the remaining 91.75 percent of US households do not.

The SEC defines an accredited investor in Rule 501 as:

1. A person who has individual net worth, or joint net worth with the person's spouse, over $1 million, excluding the value of the primary residence; or

2. A person with income over $200,000 (or $300,000 together with a spouse) in each of the two most recent years and has a reasonable expectation of the same income level in the current year; or

3. A bank, insurance company, registered investment company, business development company, or

4. A small business investment company; or an employee benefit plan, within the meaning of the Employee Retirement Income Security Act, if a bank, insurance company, or registered investment adviser makes the

---

[1] Federal Reserve SCF microdata

investment decisions, or if the plan has total assets in excess of $5 million; or

5. A charitable organization, corporation, or partnership with assets exceeding $5 million; or

6. A director, executive officer, or general partner of the company selling the securities; or

7. An entity in which all the equity owners are accredited investors; or

8. A trust with assets in excess of $5 million, not formed specifically to acquire the securities offered, whose purchases are directed by a sophisticated person.

APPENDIX III

TO 1031 EXCHANGE OR NOT TO 1031 EXCHANGE?

EXAMPLE OF EQUITY OVER TIME WITH AND WITHOUT 1031 EXCHANGE

	PERFORM 1031 EXCHANGES		DO NOT PERFORM 1031 EXCHANGES	
BUY PROPERTY A	**TOTAL**	**EQUITY**	**TOTAL**	**EQUITY**
COST	$2,800,000	$1,400,000	$2,005,000	$1,002,500
LOAN	$1,400,000		$1,002,500	
PROPERTY A SALES PRICE 5 YRS LATER	$3,245,967		$2,324,345	
COSTS OF SALE (5%)	$162,298		$116,217	
NET PROCEEDS	$1,683,669		$1,205,627	
CAPITAL GAIN (SIMPLIFIED)	$283,669		$203,127	
CAPITAL GAINS TAX (30%)	$0		$60,938	
PROCEEDS AFTER TAX	$1,683,669		$1,144,689	
BUY PROPERTY B	**TOTAL**	**EQUITY**	**TOTAL**	**EQUITY**
COST	$3,367,338	$1,683,669	$2,289,378	$1,144,689
LOAN	$1,683,669		$1,144,689	
PROPERTY B SALES PRICE 5 YRS LATER	$3,903,668		$2,654,017	
COSTS OF SALE (5%)	$195,183		$132,701	
NET PROCEEDS	$2,024,815		$1,376,627	
CAPITAL GAIN (SIMPLIFIED)	$341,146		$231,938	
CAPITAL GAINS TAX (30%)	$0		$69,581	
PROCEEDS AFTER TAX	$2,024,815		$1,307,046	

IRS Revenue Procedure 2002-22 document

Part III

Administrative, Procedural, and Miscellaneous

26 CFR 601.201: Rulings and determination letters.
(Also Part I, §§ 267, 511, 512, 707, 761, 856, 1031, 1361; 1.761-1, 1.761-2; 301.7701-1, 301.7701-2, 301.7701-3, 301.7701-4.)

Rev. Proc. 2002-22

SECTION 1. PURPOSE

This revenue procedure specifies the conditions under which the Internal Revenue Service will consider a request for a ruling that an undivided fractional interest in rental Real property (other than a mineral property as defined in section 614) is not an interest in a business entity, within the meaning of § 301.7701-2(a) of the Procedure and Administration Regulations.

This revenue procedure supersedes Rev. Proc. 2000-46, 2002-2 C.B. 438, which provides that the Service will not issue advance rulings or determination letters on the questions of whether an undivided fractional interest in real property is an interest in an entity that is not eligible for tax-free exchange under § 1031(a)(1) of the Internal Revenue Code and whether arrangements where taxpayers acquire undivided fractional interests in real property constitute separate entities for federal tax purposes under § 7701. This revenue procedure also modifies Rev. Proc. 2002-3, 2002-1 I.R.B. 117, by removing these issues from the list of subjects on which the Service will not rule. Requests for advance rulings described in Rev. Proc. 2000-46 that are not covered by this revenue procedure, such as rulings concerning mineral property, will be considered under procedures set forth in Rev. Proc. 2002-1, 2002-1 I.R.B. 1 (or its successor).

SECTION 2. BACKGROUND

Section 301.7701-1(a)(1) provides that whether an organization is an entity separate from its owners for federal tax purposes is a matter of federal law and does not depend on whether the entity is recognized as an entity under local law.

Section 301.7701-1(a)(2) provides that a joint venture or other contractual arrangement may create a separate entity for federal tax purposes if the participants carry on a trade, business, financial operation, or venture and divide the profits therefrom, but the mere co-ownership of property that is maintained, kept in repair, and rented or leased does not constitute a separate entity for federal tax purposes.

Section 301.7701-2(a) provides that a business entity is any entity recognized for federal tax purposes (including an entity with a single owner that may be disregarded as an entity separate from its owner under § 301.7701-3) that is not properly classified as a trust under § 301.7701-4 or otherwise subject to special treatment under the Internal Revenue Code. A business entity with two or more members is classified for federal tax purposes as either a corporation or a partnership.

Section 761(a) provides that the term "partnership" includes a syndicate, group, pool, joint venture, or other unincorporated organization through or by means of which any business, financial operation, or venture is carried on, and that is not a corporation or a trust or estate.

142

Section 1.761-1(a) of the Income Tax Regulations provides that the term "partnership" means a partnership as determined under §§ 301.7701-1, 301.7701-2, and 301.7701-3.

The central characteristic of a tenancy in common, one of the traditional concurrent estates in land, is that each owner is deemed to own individually a physically undivided part of the entire parcel of property. Each tenant in common is entitled to share with the other tenants the possession of the whole parcel and has the associated rights to a proportionate share of rents or profits from the property, to transfer the interest, and to demand a partition of the property. These rights generally provide a tenant in common the benefits of ownership of the property within the constraint that no rights may be exercised to the detriment of the other tenants in common. 7 Richard R. Powell, Powell on Real Property §§ 50.01-50.07 (Michael Allan Wolf ed., 2000).

Rev. Rul. 75-374, 1975-2 C.B. 261, concludes that a two-person co-ownership of an apartment building that was rented to tenants did not constitute a partnership for federal tax purposes. In the revenue ruling, the co-owners employed an agent to manage the apartments on their behalf; the agent collected rents, paid property taxes, insurance premiums, repair and maintenance expenses, and provided the tenants with customary services, such as heat, air conditioning, trash removal, unattended parking, and maintenance of public areas. The ruling concludes that the agent's activities in providing customary services to the tenants, although imputed to the co-owners, were not sufficiently extensive to cause the co-ownership to be characterized as a partnership. See also Rev. Rul. 79-77, 1979-1 C.B. 448, which did not find a business entity where three individuals transferred ownership of a commercial building subject to a net lease to a trust with the three individuals as beneficiaries.

Where a Sponsor packages co-ownership interests for sale by acquiring property, negotiating a master lease on the property, and arranging for financing, the courts have looked at the relationships not only among the co-owners, but also between the Sponsor (or persons related to the Sponsor) and the co-owners in determining whether the co-ownership gives rise to a partnership. For example, in Bergford v. Commissioner, 12 F.3d 166 (9th Cir. 1993), seventy-eight investors purchased "co-ownership" interests in computer equipment that was subject to a 7-year net lease. As part of the purchase, the co-owners authorized the manager to arrange financing and refinancing, purchase and lease the equipment, collect rents and apply those rents to the notes used to finance the equipment, prepare statements, and advance funds to participants on an interest-free basis to meet cash flow. The agreement allowed the co-owners to decide by majority vote whether to sell or lease the equipment at the end of the lease. Absent a majority vote, the manager could make that decision. In addition, the manager was entitled to a remarketing fee of 10 percent of the equipment's selling price or lease rental whether or not a co-owner terminated the agreement or the manager performed any remarketing. A co-owner could assign an interest in the co-ownership only after fulfilling numerous conditions and obtaining the manager's consent.

The court held that the co-ownership arrangement constituted a partnership for federal tax purposes. Among the factors that influenced the court's decision were the limitations on the co-owners' ability to sell, lease, or encumber either the co-ownership interest or the underlying property, and the manager's effective participation in both profits (through the remarketing fee) and losses (through the advances). Bergford, 12 F.3d at 169-170. Accord Bussing v. Commissioner, 88 T.C.

449 (1987), aff'd on reh'g, 89 T.C. 1050 (1987); Alhouse v. Commissioner, T.C. Memo. 1991-652. Under § 1.761-1(a) and §§ 301.7701-1 through 301.7701-3, a federal tax partnership does not include mere co-ownership of property where the owners' activities are limited to keeping the property maintained, in repair, rented or leased. However, as the above authorities demonstrate, a partnership for federal tax purposes is broader in scope than the common law meaning of partnership and may include groups not classified by state law as partnerships. Bergford, 12 F.3d at 169. Where the parties to a venture join together capital or services with the intent of conducting a business or enterprise and of sharing the profits and losses from the venture, a partnership (or other business entity) is created. Bussing, 88 T.C. at 460. Furthermore, where the economic benefits to the individual participants are not derivative of their co-ownership, but rather come from their joint relationship toward a common goal, the co-ownership arrangement will be characterized as a partnership (or other business entity) for federal tax purposes. Bergford, 12 F.3d at 169.

SECTION 3. SCOPE

This revenue procedure applies to co-ownership of rental real property (other than mineral interests) (the Property) in an arrangement classified under local law as a tenancy-in-common.

This revenue procedure provides guidelines for requesting advance rulings solely to assist taxpayers in preparing ruling requests and the Service in issuing advance ruling letters as promptly as practicable. The guidelines set forth in this revenue procedure are not intended to be substantive rules and are not to be used for audit purposes.

SECTION 4. GUIDELINES FOR SUBMITTING RULING REQUESTS

The Service ordinarily will not consider a request for a ruling under this revenue procedure unless the information described in section 5 of this revenue procedure is included in the ruling request and the conditions described in section 6 of this revenue procedure are satisfied. Even if sections 5 and 6 of this revenue procedure are satisfied, however, the Service may decline to issue a ruling under this revenue procedure whenever warranted by the facts and circumstances of a particular case and whenever appropriate in the interest of sound tax administration.

Where multiple parcels of property owned by the co-owners are leased to a single tenant pursuant to a single lease agreement and any debt of one or more co-owners is secured by all of the parcels, the Service will generally treat all of the parcels as a single "Property." In such a case, the Service will generally not consider a ruling request under this revenue procedure unless: (1) each co-owner's percentage interest in each parcel is identical to that co-owner's percentage interest in every other parcel, (2) each co-owner's percentage interests in the parcels cannot be separated and traded independently, and (3) the parcels of property are properly viewed as a single business unit. The Service will generally treat contiguous parcels as comprising a single business unit. Even if the parcels are not contiguous, however, the Service may treat multiple parcels as comprising a single business unit where there is a close connection between the business use of one parcel and the business use of another parcel. For example, an office building and a garage that services the tenants of the office building may be treated as a single business unit even if the office building and the garage are not contiguous.

For purposes of this revenue procedure, the following definitions apply. The term "co-owner" means any person that owns an interest in the Property as a tenant in common. The term "Sponsor" means any person who divides a single interest in the Property into multiple co-ownership interests for the purpose of offering those interests for sale. The term "related person" means a person bearing a relationship described in § 267(b) or 707(b)(1), except that in applying § 267(b) or 707(b)(1), the co-ownership will be treated as a partnership and each co-owner will be treated as a partner. The term "disregarded entity" means an entity that is disregarded as an entity separate from its owner for federal tax purposes. Examples of disregarded entities include qualified REIT subsidiaries (within the meaning of § 856(i)(2)), qualified subchapter S subsidiaries (within the meaning of § 1361(b)(3)(B)), and business entities that have only one owner and do not elect to be classified as corporations. The term "blanket lien" means any mortgage or trust deed that is recorded against the Property as a whole.

SECTION 5. INFORMATION TO BE SUBMITTED

.01 Section 8 of Rev. Proc. 2002-1 outlines general requirements concerning the information to be submitted as part of a ruling request, including advance rulings under this revenue procedure. For example, any ruling request must contain a complete statement of all facts relating to the co-ownership, including those relating to promoting, financing, and managing the Property. Among the information to be included are the items of information specified in this revenue procedure; therefore, the ruling request must provide all items of information and conditions specified below and in section 6 of this revenue procedure, or at least account for all of the items. For example, if a co-ownership arrangement has no brokerage agreement permitted in section

6.12 of this revenue procedure, the ruling request should so state. Furthermore, merely submitting documents and supplementary materials required by section 5.02 of this revenue procedure does not satisfy all of the information requirements contained in section 5.02 of this revenue procedure or in section 8 of Rev. Proc. 2002-1; all material facts in the documents submitted must be explained in the ruling request and may not be merely incorporated by reference. All submitted documents and supplementary materials must contain applicable exhibits, attachments, and amendments. The ruling request must identify and explain any information or documents required in section 5 of this revenue procedure that are not included and any conditions in section 6 of this revenue procedure that are or are not satisfied.

.02 Required General Information and Copies of Documents and Supplementary Materials. Generally the following information and copies of documents and materials must be submitted with the ruling request:

(1) The name, taxpayer identification number, and percentage fractional interest in Property of each co-owner;

(2) The name, taxpayer identification number, ownership of, and any relationship among, all persons involved in the acquisition, sale, lease and other use of Property, including the Sponsor, lessee, manager, and lender;

(3) A full description of the Property;

(4) A representation that each of the co-owners holds title to the Property (including each of multiple parcels of property treated as a single Property under this revenue procedure) as a tenant in common under local law;

(5) All promotional documents relating to the sale of fractional interests in the Property;

(6) All lending agreements relating to the Property;

(7) All agreements among the co-owners relating to the Property;

(8) Any lease agreement relating to the Property;

(9) Any purchase and sale agreement relating to the Property;

(10) Any property management or brokerage agreement relating to the Property; and

(11) Any other agreement relating to the Property not specified in this section, including agreements relating to any debt secured by the Property (such as guarantees or indemnity agreements) and any call and put options relating to the Property.

SECTION 6. CONDITIONS FOR OBTAINING RULINGS

The Service ordinarily will not consider a request for a ruling under this revenue procedure unless the conditions described below are satisfied. Nevertheless, where the conditions described below are not satisfied, the Service may consider a request for a ruling under this revenue procedure where the facts and circumstances clearly establish that such a ruling is appropriate.

.01 Tenancy in Common Ownership. Each of the co-owners must hold title to the Property (either directly or through a disregarded entity) as a tenant in common under local law. Thus, title to the Property as a whole may not be held by an entity recognized under local law.

.02 Number of Co-Owners. The number of co-owners must be limited to no more than 35 persons. For this purpose, "person" is defined as in § 7701(a)(1), except that a husband and wife are treated as a single person and all persons who acquire interests from a co-owner by inheritance are treated as a single person.

.03 No Treatment of Co-Ownership as an Entity. The co-ownership may not file a partnership or corporate tax return, conduct business under a common name, execute an agreement identifying any or all of the co-owners as partners, shareholders, or members of a business entity, or otherwise hold itself out as a partnership or other form of business entity (nor may the co-owners hold themselves out as partners, shareholders, or members of a business entity). The Service generally will not issue a ruling under this revenue procedure if the co-owners held interests in the Property through a partnership or corporation immediately prior to the formation of the co-ownership.

.04 Co-Ownership Agreement. The co-owners may enter into a limited co-ownership agreement that may run with the land. For example, a co-ownership agreement may provide that a co-owner must offer the co-ownership interest for sale to the other co-owners, the Sponsor, or the lessee at fair market value (determined as of the time the partition right is exercised) before exercising any right to partition (see section 6.06 of this revenue procedure for conditions relating to restrictions on alienation); or that certain actions on behalf of the co-ownership require the vote of co-owners holding more than 50 percent of the undivided interests in the Property (see section 6.05 of this revenue procedure for conditions relating to voting).

.05 Voting. The co-owners must retain the right to approve the hiring of any manager, the sale or other disposition of the Property, any leases of a portion or all of the Property, or the creation or modification of a blanket lien. Any sale, lease, or re-lease of a portion or all of the Property, any negotiation or renegotiation of indebtedness secured by a blanket lien, the hiring of any manager, or the negotiation of any management contract (or any extension or renewal of such contract) must be by unanimous approval of the co-owners. For all other actions on behalf of the co-ownership, the co-owners may agree to be bound by the vote of those holding more than 50 percent of the undivided interests in the Property. A co-owner who has consented to an action in conformance with this section 6.05 may provide the manager or other person a power of attorney to execute a specific document with respect to that action, but may not provide the manager or other person with a global power of attorney.

.06 Restrictions on Alienation. In general, each co-owner must have the rights to transfer, partition, and encumber the co-owner's undivided interest in the Property without the agreement or approval of any person. However, restrictions on the right to transfer, partition, or encumber interests in the Property that are required by a lender and that are consistent with customary commercial lending practices are not prohibited. See section 6.14 of this revenue procedure for restrictions on who may be a lender. Moreover, the co-owners, the Sponsor, or the lessee may have a right of first offer (the right to have the first opportunity to offer to purchase the co-ownership interest) with respect to any co-owner's exercise of the right to transfer the co-ownership interest in the Property. In addition, a co-owner may agree to offer the co-ownership interest for sale to the other co-owners, the Sponsor, or the lessee at fair market value (determined as of the time the partition right is exercised) before exercising any right to partition.

.07 Sharing Proceeds and Liabilities upon Sale of Property. If the Property is sold, any debt secured by a blanket lien must be satisfied and the remaining sales proceeds must be distributed to the co-owners.

.08 Proportionate Sharing of Profits and Losses. Each co-owner must share in all revenues generated by the Property and all costs associated with the Property in proportion to the co-owner's undivided interest in the Property. Neither the other co-owners, nor the Sponsor, nor the manager may advance funds to a co-owner to meet expenses associated with the co-ownership interest, unless the advance is recourse to the co-owner (and, where the co-owner is a disregarded entity, the owner of the co-owner) and is not for a period exceeding 31 days.

.09 Proportionate Sharing of Debt. The co-owners must share in any indebtedness secured by a blanket lien in proportion to their undivided interests.

.10 Options. A co-owner may issue an option to purchase the co-owner's undivided interest (call option), provided that the exercise price for the call option reflects the fair market value of the Property determined as of the time the option is exercised. For this purpose, the fair market value of an undivided interest in the Property is equal to the co-owner's percentage interest in the Property multiplied by the fair market value of the Property as a whole. A co-owner may not acquire an option to sell the co-owner's undivided interest (put option) to the Sponsor, the lessee, another co-owner, or the lender, or any person related to the Sponsor, the lessee, another co-owner, or the lender.

.11 No Business Activities. The co-owners' activities must be limited to those customarily performed in connection with the maintenance and repair of rental real property (customary activities). See Rev. Rul. 75-374, 1975-2 C.B. 261. Activities will be treated as customary activities for this purpose if the activities would not prevent an amount received by an organization described in § 511(a)(2) from qualifying as rent under § 512(b)(3) (A) and the regulations thereunder. In determining the co-owners' activities, all activities of the co-owners, their agents, and any persons related to the co-owners with respect to the Property will be taken into account, whether or not those activities are performed by the co-owners in their capacities as co-owners. For example, if the Sponsor or a lessee is a co-owner, then all of the activities of the Sponsor or lessee (or any person related to the Sponsor or lessee) with respect to the Property will be taken into account in determining whether the co-owners' activities are customary activities. However, activities of a co-owner or a related person with respect to the Property (other than in the co-owner's capacity as a co-owner) will not be taken into account if the co-owner owns an undivided interest in the Property for less than 6 months.

.12 Management and Brokerage Agreements. The co-owners may enter into management or brokerage agreements, which must be renewable no less frequently than annually, with an agent, who may be the Sponsor or a co-owner (or any person related to the Sponsor or a co-owner), but who may not be a lessee. The management agreement may authorize the manager to maintain a common bank account for the collection and deposit of rents and to offset expenses associated with the Property against any revenues before disbursing each co-owner's share of net revenues. In all events, however, the manager must disburse to the co-owners their shares of net revenues within 3 months from the date of receipt of those revenues. The management agreement may also authorize the manager to prepare statements for the co-owners showing their shares of revenue and costs from the Property. In addition, the management agreement may authorize the manager to obtain or modify insurance on the Property, and to negotiate modifications of the terms of any lease or any indebtedness encumbering the Property, subject to the approval of the co-owners. (See section 6.05 of this revenue procedure for conditions relating to the approval of lease and debt modifications.) The determination of any fees paid by the co-ownership to the manager must not depend in whole or in part on the income or profits derived by any person from the Property and may not exceed the fair market value of the manager's services. Any fee paid by the co-ownership to a broker must be comparable to fees paid by unrelated parties to brokers for similar services.

.13 Leasing Agreements. All leasing arrangements must be bona fide leases for federal tax purposes. Rents paid by a lessee must reflect the fair market value for the use of the Property. The determination of the amount of the rent must not depend, in whole or in part, on the income or profits derived by any person from the Property leased (other than an amount based on a fixed percentage or percentages of receipts or sales). See section 856(d)(2)(A) and the regulations thereunder. Thus, for example, the amount of rent paid by a lessee may not be based on a percentage of net income from the Property, cash flow, increases in equity, or similar arrangements.

.14 Loan Agreements. The lender with respect to any debt that encumbers the Property or with respect to any debt incurred to acquire an undivided interest in the Property may not be a related person to any co-owner, the Sponsor, the manager, or any lessee of the Property.

.15 Payments to Sponsor. Except as otherwise provided in this revenue procedure, the amount of any payment to the Sponsor for the acquisition of the co-ownership interest (and the amount of any fees paid to the Sponsor for services) must reflect the fair market value of the acquired co-ownership interest (or the services rendered) and may not depend, in whole or in part, on the income or profits derived by any person from the Property.

SECTION 6. EFFECT ON OTHER DOCUMENTS

Rev. Proc. 2000-46 is superseded. Rev. Proc. 2002-3 is modified by removing sections 5.03 and 5.06. SECTION 7. DRAFTING INFORMATION The principal authors of this revenue procedure are Jeanne Sullivan and Deane Burke of the Office of Associate Chief Counsel (Passthroughs and Special Industries). For further information regarding this revenue procedure, contact Ms. Sullivan or Mr. Burke at (202) 622-3070 (not a toll-free call).

APPENDIX V

SIMPLIFIED 25 YEAR ILLUSTRATION OF DEPRECIATION BUILDUP ANDCUMULATIVE EQUITY GAINED IN SEQUENTIAL 1031 EXCHANGES

1. Buy a Palo Alto Duplex
2. 10 Years Later, Exchange All Cash Out to Buy a DST with 50% LTV
3. 7.5 Years Later, Sell Your DST, Use All Cash Out to Buy Another DST With 50% LTV

Assume you perform full exchanges (no cash out) and buy DSTs with a 50% LTV using all your cash from the previous sale.
Assume DST properties 80% are improvements When Purchased
Assume 35% capital gains tax rate
Assume DST properties are all multifamily

FIRST INVESTMENT PROPERTY IN PALO ALTO DUPLEX: PROPERTY A

Year 1	Property A purchase price	$1,000,000
	Down Payment (equity)	$500,000
	Original Loan	$500,000
	Original LTV	50%
	Annual Depreciation Expense for 30 Years	$16,667
	Number Of Years Held	10
	Sale Price After Expenses	$1,829,451
	(Assume 7% Appreciation, 6% Expenses)	
	Debt on Property at Sale	$408,773
	Equity from Sale	$1,420,678
	LTV at Sale	22%
	Capital Gains Tax Due With Even 1031 Exchange	0
	Capital Gain From Sale	$420,678
	Taxes that would have been due at sale	
	without a 1031 exchange (35% tax rate assumed)	$147,237
	# Years Left On Property A Depreciation	
	Schedule at $16,667 per Year	20
	Requirement in Purchase Value	
Year 10	For Even 1031 Exchange	$1,829,451

1031 EXCHANGE AND PURCHASE MULTIFAMILY DST: PROPERTY B

Year 10	Property B purchase price	$2,841,356
	Equity From Sale of A Property	$1,420,678
	Assumed Debt	$1,420,678
	LTV at Purchase	50%
	Amount of Property Purchased Over 1031 Exchange Requirement (New Depreciation Schedule)	$1,011,905
	Property B New Annual Depreciation Expense For 30 Years	$26,984
	Property A Old Depreciation Expense For 20 More Years	$16,667
	Total Depreciation	$43,651
	Number Of Years Held	7.5
	Sale Price After Expenses (Assume 2% Appreciation)	$3,296,301
	Debt Balance Due at sale (Assume 2% Principal Pay Down)	$1,338,258
	Equity from Sale of B Property	$1,958,043
	LTV at Sale	41%
	Capital Gains Tax Due With Even 1031 Exchange	0
	Capital Gain From Sale	$1,284,396
	Taxes that would have been due at sale without a 1031 exchange (35% tax rate assumed)	$449,539
	# Years Left On Property A Depreciation Schedule at $16,667 per Year	12.5
	# Years Left On Property B Depreciation Schedule at $26,984 per Year	22.5
Year 17.5	Required Purchase Price For Even 1031 Exchange (Equity + Loan Balance)	$3,296,301

1031 EXCHANGE AND PURCHASE MULTIFAMILY DST: PROPERTY C

Year 17.5	Property C purchase price	$3,916,086
	Equity From Sale of B Property	$1,958,043
	Assumed Debt	$1,958,043
	LTV at Purchase	50%
	Amount of Property Purchased Over 1031 Exchange Requirement (New Depreciation Schedule)	$619,785
	Property C New Annual Depreciation Expense For 30 Years	$16,528
	Property B Old Depreciation Expense For 20 More Years	$26,984
	Property A Old Depreciation Expense For 5 More Years	$16,667
	Total Depreciation	$60,178
	Number Of Years Held	7.5
	Sale Price After Expenses (Assume 2% Appreciation)	$4,543,113
	Debt Balance Due at sale (Assume 2% Principal Pay Down)	$1,856,873
	Equity from Sale of C Property	$2,686,240
	LTV at Sale	41%
	Capital Gains Tax Due With Even 1031 Exchange	0
	Capital Gain From Sale	$1,911,423
	Taxes that would have been due at sale without a 1031 exchange (35% tax rate assumed)	$668,998
	# Years Left On Property A Depreciation Schedule at $16,667 per Year	5
	# Years Left On Property B Depreciation Schedule at $26,984 per Year	15
Year 25	# Years Left On Property C Depreciation Schedule at $16,528 per Year	22.5
	Required Purchase Price For Even 1031 Exchange (Equity + Loan Balance)	$4,543,113

Passco Lone Oak DST, Austin, TX, is a multifamily apartment property. In this central courtyard, a beautiful waterfall and regulation sized pool are the centerpiece of tenant gatherings.

Materials & Resources

Internal Revenue Bulletin: 2004-33
August 16, 2004
Rev. Rul. 2004-86

Classification of Delaware statutory trust. This ruling explains how a Delaware statutory trust described in the ruling will be classified for federal tax purposes and whether a taxpayer may acquire an interest in the Delaware statutory trust without recognition of gain or loss under section 1031 of the Code. Rev. Ruls. 78-371 and 92-105 distinguished.

ISSUE(S)

(1) In the situation described below, how is a Delaware statutory trust, described in Del. Code Ann. title 12, §§ 3801 - 3824, classified for federal tax purposes?

(2) In the situation described below, may a taxpayer exchange real property for an interest in a Delaware statutory trust without recognition of gain or loss under § 1031 of the Internal Revenue Code?

FACTS

On January 1, 2005, *A*, an individual, borrows money from *BK*, a bank, and signs a 10-year note bearing adequate stated interest, within the meaning of § 483.On January 1, 2005, *A* uses the proceeds of the loan to purchase Blackacre, rental real property. The note is secured by Blackacre and is nonrecourse to *A*.

Immediately following *A*'s purchase of Blackacre, *A* enters into a net lease with *Z* for a term of 10 years. Under the terms of the lease, *Z* is to pay all taxes, assessments, fees, or other charges imposed on Blackacre by federal, state, or local authorities. In addition, *Z* is to pay all insurance, maintenance, ordinary repairs, and utilities relating to Blackacre. *Z* may sublease Blackacre. *Z*'s rent is a fixed amount that may be adjusted by a formula described in the lease agreement that is based upon a fixed rate or an objective index, such as an escalator clause based upon the Consumer Price Index, but adjustments to the rate or index are not within the control of any of the parties to the lease. *Z*'s rent is not contingent on *Z*'s ability to lease the property or on *Z*'s gross sales or net profits derived from the property.

Also on January 1, 2005, *A* forms *DST*, a Delaware statutory trust described in the Delaware Statutory Trust Act, Del. Code Ann. title 12, §§ 3801 - 3824, to hold property for investment. *A* contributes Blackacre to *DST*. Upon contribution, *DST* assumes *A*'s rights and obligations under the note with *BK* and the lease with *Z*. In accordance with the terms of the note, neither *DST* nor any of its beneficial owners are personally liable to *BK* on the note, which continues to be secured by Blackacre.

The trust agreement provides that interests in *DST* are freely transferable. However, *DST* interests are not publicly traded on an established securities market. *DST* will terminate on the earlier of 10 years from the date of its creation or the disposition of Blackacre, but will not terminate on the bankruptcy, death, or incapacity of any owner or on the transfer of any right, title, or interest of the owners. The trust agreement further provides that interests in *DST* will be of a single class, representing undivided beneficial interests in the assets of *DST*.

Under the trust agreement, the trustee is authorized to establish a reasonable reserve for expenses associated with holding Blackacre that may be payable out of trust funds. The trustee is required to distribute all available cash less reserves quarterly to each beneficial owner in proportion to their respective interests in *DST*. The trustee is required to invest cash received from Blackacre between each quarterly distribution and all cash held in reserve in short-term obligations of (or guaranteed by) the United States, or any agency or instrumentality thereof, and in certificates of deposit of any bank or trust company having a minimum stated surplus and capital. The trustee is permitted to invest only in obligations maturing prior to the next distribution date and is required to hold such obligations until maturity. In addition to the right to a quarterly distribution of cash, each beneficial owner has the right to an in-kind distribution of its proportionate share of trust property.

The trust agreement provides that the trustee's activities are limited to the collection and distribution of income. The trustee may not exchange Blackacre for other property, purchase assets other than the short-term investments described above, or accept additional contributions of assets (including money) to *DST*. The trustee may not renegotiate the terms of the debt used to acquire Blackacre and may not renegotiate the lease with *Z* or enter into leases with tenants other than *Z*, except in the case of *Z*'s bankruptcy or insolvency. In addition, the trustee may make only minor non-structural modifications to Blackacre, unless otherwise required by law. The trust agreement further provides that the trustee may engage in ministerial activities to the extent required to maintain and operate *DST* under local law.

On January 3, 2005, *B* and *C* exchange Whiteacre and Greenacre, respectively, for all of *A*'s interests in *DST* through a Qualified Intermediary, within the meaning of § 1.1031(k)-1(g). *A* does not engage in a § 1031 exchange. Whiteacre and Greenacre were held for investment and are of like kind to Blackacre, within the meaning of § 1031.

Neither *DST* nor its trustee enters into a written agreement with *A*, *B*, or *C*, creating an agency relationship. In dealings with third parties, neither *DST* nor its trustee is represented as an agent of *A*, *B*, or *C*.

BK is not related to *A*, *B*, *C*, *DST*'s trustee or *Z* within the meaning of § 267(b) or § 707(b). *Z* is not related to *B*, *C*, or *DST*'s trustee within the meaning of § 267(b) or § 707(b).

LAW

Delaware law provides that a Delaware statutory trust is an unincorporated association recognized as an entity separate from its owners. A Delaware statutory trust is created by executing a governing instrument and filing an executed certificate of trust. Creditors of the beneficial owners of a Delaware statutory trust may not assert claims directly against the property in the trust. A Delaware statutory trust may sue or be sued, and property held in a Delaware statutory trust is subject to attachment or execution as if the trust were a corporation. Beneficial owners of a Delaware statutory trust are entitled to the same limitation on personal liability because of actions of the Delaware statutory trust that is extended to stockholders of Delaware corporations. A Delaware statutory trust may merge or consolidate with or into one or more statutory entities or other business entities.

Section 671 provides that, where the grantor or another person is treated as the owner of any portion of a trust (commonly referred to as a "grantor trust"), there shall be included in computing the taxable income and credits of the grantor or the other person those items of income, deductions, and credits against tax of the trust which are attributable to that portion of the trust to the extent that the items would be taken into account under chapter

1 in computing taxable income or credits against the tax of an individual.

Section 1.671-2(e)(1) of the Income Tax Regulations provides that, for purposes of subchapter J, a grantor includes any person to the extent such person either creates a trust or directly or indirectly makes a gratuitous transfer of property to a trust.

Under § 1.671-2(e)(3), the term "grantor" includes any person who acquires an interest in a trust from a grantor of the trust if the interest acquired is an interest in certain investment trusts described in § 301.7701-4(c).

Under § 677(a), the grantor is treated as the owner of any portion of a trust whose income without the approval or consent of any adverse party is, or, in the discretion of the grantor or a nonadverse party, or both, may be distributed, or held or accumulated for future distribution, to the grantor or the grantor's spouse.

A person that is treated as the owner of an undivided fractional interest of a trust under subpart E of part I, subchapter J of the Code (§§ 671 and following), is considered to own the trust assets attributable to that undivided fractional interest of the trust for federal income tax purposes. *See* Rev. Rul. 88-103, 1988-2 C.B. 304; Rev. Rul. 85-45, 1985-1 C.B. 183; and Rev. Rul. 85-13, 1985-1 C.B. 184. *See also* § 1.1001-2(c), *Example* 5.

Section 761(a) provides that the term "partnership" includes a syndicate, group, pool, joint venture, or other unincorporated organization through or by means of which any business, financial operation, or venture is carried on, and that is not a corporation or a trust or estate. Under regulations the Secretary may, at the election of all the members of the unincorporated organization, exclude such organization from the application of all or part of subchapter K, if the income of the members of the organization may be adequately determined without the computation of partnership taxable income and the organization is availed of (1) for investment purposes only and not for the active conduct of a business, (2) for the joint production, extraction, or use of property, but not for the purpose of selling services or property produced or extracted, or (3) by dealers in securities for a short period for the purpose of underwriting, selling, or distributing a particular issue of securities.

Section 1.761-2(a)(2) provides the requirements that must be satisfied for participants in the joint purchase, retention, sale, or exchange of investment property to elect to be excluded from the application of the provisions of subchapter K. One of these requirements is that the participants own the property as coowners.

Section 1031(a)(1) provides that no gain or loss is recognized on the exchange of property held for productive use in a trade or business or for investment if such property is exchanged solely for property of like kind that is to be held either for productive use in a trade or business or for investment.

Section 1031(a)(2) provides that § 1031(a) does not apply to any exchange of stocks, bonds or notes, other securities or evidences of indebtedness or interest, interests in a partnership, or certificates of trust or beneficial interests. It further provides that an interest in a partnership that has in effect a valid election under § 761(a) to be excluded from the application of all of subchapter K shall be treated as an interest in each of the assets of the partnership and not as an interest in a partnership.

Under § 301.7701-1(a)(1) of the Procedure and Administration Regulations, whether an organization is an entity separate from

167

its owners for federal tax purposes is a matter of federal tax law and does not depend on whether the organization is recognized as an entity under local law.

Generally, when participants in a venture form a state law entity and avail themselves of the benefits of that entity for a valid business purpose, such as investment or profit, and not for tax avoidance, the entity will be recognized for federal tax purposes. *See Moline Properties, Inc. v. Comm'r,* 319 U.S. 436 (1943); *Zmuda v. Comm'r,* 731 F.2d 1417 (9th Cir. 1984); *Boca Investerings P'ship v. United States,* 314 F.3d 625 (D.C. Cir. 2003); *Saba P'ship v. Comm'r,* 273 F.3d 1135 (D.C. Cir. 2001); *ASA Investerings P'ship v. Comm'r,* 201 F.3d 505 (D.C. Cir. 2000); *Markosian v. Comm'r,* 73 T.C. 1235 (1980).

Section 301.7701-2(a) defines the term "business entity" as any entity recognized for federal tax purposes (including an entity with a single owner that may be disregarded as an entity separate from its owner under § 301.7701-3) that is not properly classified as a trust under § 301.7701-4 or otherwise subject to special treatment under the Code. A business entity with two or more owners is classified for federal tax purposes as either a corporation or a partnership. A business entity with only one owner is classified as a corporation or is disregarded.

Section 301.7701-3(a) provides that an eligible entity can elect its classification for federal tax purposes. Under § 301.7701-3(b)(1), unless the entity elects otherwise, a domestic eligible entity is a partnership if it has two or more owners or is disregarded as an entity separate from its owner if it has a single owner.

Section 301.7701-4(a) provides that the term "trust" refers to an arrangement created either by will or by an inter vivos declaration whereby trustees take title to property for the purpose of protecting and conserving it for the beneficiaries. Usually the beneficiaries of a trust do no more than accept the benefits thereof and are not voluntary planners or creators of the trust arrangement. However, the beneficiaries of a trust may be the persons who create it, and it will be recognized as a trust if it was created for the purpose of protecting and conserving the trust property for beneficiaries who stand in the same relation to the trust as they would if the trust had been created by others for them.

Section 301.7701-4(b) provides that there are other arrangements known as trusts because the legal title to property is conveyed to trustees for the benefit of beneficiaries, but that are not classified as trusts for federal tax purposes because they are not simply arrangements to protect or conserve the property for the beneficiaries. These trusts, which are often known as business or commercial trusts, generally are created by the beneficiaries simply as a device to carry on a profit-making business that normally would have been carried on through business organizations that are classified as corporations or partnerships.

Section 301.7701-4(c)(1) provides that an "investment" trust will not be classified as a trust if there is a power under the trust agreement to vary the investment of the certificate holders. *See Comm'r v. North American Bond Trust*, 122 F.2d 545 (2d Cir. 1941), *cert. denied*, 314 U.S. 701 (1942). An investment trust with a single class of ownership interests, representing undivided beneficial interests in the assets of the trust, will be classified as a trust if there is no power to vary the investment of the certificate holders.

A power to vary the investment of the certificate holders exists where there is a managerial power, under the trust instrument, that enables a trust to take advantage of variations in the market to improve the investment of the investors. *See Comm'r v. North American Bond Trust,* 122 F.2d at 546.

Rev. Rul. 75-192, 1975-1 C.B. 384, discusses the situation where a provision in the trust agreement requires the trustee to invest cash on hand between the quarterly distribution dates. The trustee is required to invest the money in short-term obligations of (or guaranteed by) the United States, or any agency or instrumentality thereof, and in certificates of deposit of any bank or trust company having a minimum stated surplus and capital. The trustee is permitted to invest only in obligations maturing prior to the next distribution date and is required to hold such obligations until maturity. Rev. Rul. 75-192 concludes that, because the restrictions on the types of permitted investments limit the trustee to a fixed return similar to that earned on a bank account and eliminate any opportunity to profit from market fluctuations, the power to invest in the specified kinds of short-term investments is not a power to vary the trust's investment.

Rev. Rul. 78-371, 1978-2 C.B. 344, concludes that a trust established by the heirs of a number of contiguous parcels of real estate is an association taxable as a corporation for federal tax purposes where the trustees have the power to purchase and sell contiguous or adjacent real estate, accept or retain contributions of contiguous or adjacent real estate, raze or erect any building or structure, make any improvements to the land originally contributed, borrow money, and mortgage or lease the property. *Compare* Rev. Rul. 79-77, 1979-1 C.B. 448 (concluding that a trust formed by three parties to hold a single parcel of real estate is classified as a trust for federal income tax purposes when the trustee has limited powers that do not evidence an intent to carry on a profit making business).

Rev. Rul. 92-105, 1992-2 C.B. 204, addresses the transfer of a taxpayer's interest in an Illinois land trust under § 1031. Under the facts of the ruling, a single taxpayer created an Illinois land trust and named a domestic corporation as trustee. Under the deed of trust, the taxpayer transferred legal and equitable title to real property to the trust, subject to the provisions of an accompanying land trust agreement. The land trust agreement provided that the taxpayer retained exclusive control of the management, operation, renting, and selling of the real property, together with an exclusive right to the earnings and proceeds from the real property. Under the agreement, the taxpayer was required to file all tax returns, pay all taxes, and satisfy any other liabilities with respect to the real property. Rev. Rul 92-105 concludes that, because the trustee's only responsibility was to hold and transfer title at the direction of the taxpayer, a trust, as defined in § 301.7701-4(a), was not established. Moreover, there were no other arrangements between the taxpayer and the trustee (or between the taxpayer and any other person) that would cause the overall arrangement to be classified as a partnership (or any other type of entity). Instead, the trustee was a mere agent for the holding and transfer of title to real property, and the taxpayer retained direct ownership of the real property for federal income tax purposes.

ANALYSIS

Under Delaware law, *DST* is an entity that is recognized as separate from its owners. Creditors of the beneficial owners of *DST* may not assert claims directly against Blackacre. *DST* may sue or be sued, and the property of *DST* is subject to attachment and execution as if it were a corporation. The beneficial owners of *DST* are entitled to the same limitation on personal liability because of actions of *DST* that is extended to stockholders of

Delaware corporations. *DST* may merge or consolidate with or into one or more statutory entities or other business entities. *DST* is formed for investment purposes. Thus, *DST* is an entity for federal tax purposes.

Whether *DST* or its trustee is an agent of *DST*'s beneficial owners depends upon the arrangement between the parties. The beneficiaries of *DST* do not enter into an agency agreement with *DST* or its trustee. Further, neither *DST* nor its trustee acts as an agent for *A*, *B*, or *C* in dealings with third parties. Thus, neither *DST* nor its trustee is the agent of *DST*'s beneficial owners. *Cf. Comm'r v. Bollinger*, 485 U.S. 340 (1988).

This situation is distinguishable from Rev. Rul. 92-105. First, in Rev. Rul. 92-105, the beneficiary retained the direct obligation to pay liabilities and taxes relating to the property. *DST*, in contrast, assumed *A*'s obligations on the lease with *Z* and on the loan with *BK*, and Delaware law provides the beneficial owners of *DST* with the same limitation on personal liability extended to shareholders of Delaware corporations. Second, unlike *A*, the beneficiary in Rev. Rul. 92-105 retained the right to manage and control the trust property.

Issue 1. Classification of Delaware Statutory Trust

Because *DST* is an entity separate from its owner, *DST* is either a trust or a business entity for federal tax purposes. To determine whether *DST* is a trust or a business entity for federal tax purposes, it is necessary, under § 301.7701-4(c)(1), to determine whether there is a power under the trust agreement to vary the investment of the certificate holders.

Prior to, but on the same date as, the transfer of Blackacre to *DST*, *A* entered into a 10-year nonrecourse loan secured by

Blackacre. *A* also entered into the 10-year net lease agreement with *Z*. *A*'s rights and obligations under the loan and lease were assumed by *DST*. Because the duration of *DST* is 10 years (unless Blackacre is disposed of prior to that time), the financing and leasing arrangements related to Blackacre that were made prior to the inception of *DST* are fixed for the entire life of *DST*. Further, the trustee may only invest in short-term obligations that mature prior to the next distribution date and is required to hold these obligations until maturity. Because the trust agreement requires that any cash from Blackacre, and any cash earned on short-term obligations held by *DST* between distribution dates, be distributed quarterly, and because the disposition of Blackacre results in the termination of *DST*, no reinvestment of such monies is possible.

The trust agreement provides that the trustee's activities are limited to the collection and distribution of income. The trustee may not exchange Blackacre for other property, purchase assets other than the short-term investments described above, or accept additional contributions of assets (including money) to *DST*. The trustee may not renegotiate the terms of the debt used to acquire Blackacre and may not renegotiate the lease with *Z* or enter into leases with tenants other than *Z*, except in the case of *Z*'s bankruptcy or insolvency. In addition, the trustee may make only minor non-structural modifications to Blackacre, unless otherwise required by law.

This situation is distinguishable from Rev. Rul. 78-371, because *DST*'s trustee has none of the powers described in Rev. Rul. 78-371, which evidence an intent to carry on a profit making business. Because all of the interests in *DST* are of a single class representing undivided beneficial interests in the assets of *DST* and *DST*'s trustee has no power to vary the investment of the certificate holders to benefit from variations in the market, *DST* is an investment trust that will be classified as a trust under § 301.7701-4(c)(1).

Issue 2. Exchange of Real Property for Interests under § 1031

B and *C* are treated as grantors of the trust under § 1.671-2(e)(3) when they acquire their interests in the trust from *A*. Because they have the right to distributions of all trust income attributable to their undivided fractional interests in the trust, *B* and *C* are each treated, by reason of § 677, as the owner of an *aliquot* portion of the trust and all income, deductions, and credits attributable to that portion are includible by *B* and *C* under § 671 in computing their taxable income. Because the owner of an undivided fractional interest of a trust is considered to own the trust assets attributable to that interest for federal income tax purposes, *B* and *C* are each considered to own an undivided fractional interest in Blackacre for federal income tax purposes. *See* Rev. Rul. 85-13.

Accordingly, the exchange of real property by *B* and *C* for an interest in *DST* through a Qualified Intermediary is the exchange of real property for an interest in Blackacre, and not the exchange of real property for a certificate of trust or beneficial interest under § 1031(a)(2)(E). Because Whiteacre and Greenacre are of like kind to Blackacre, and provided the other requirements of § 1031 are satisfied, the exchange of real property for an interest in *DST* by *B* and *C* will qualify for nonrecognition of gain or loss under § 1031. Moreover, because *DST* is a grantor trust, the outcome to the parties will remain the same, even if *A* transfers interests in Blackacre directly to *B* and *C*, and *B* and *C* immediately form *DST* by contributing their interests in Blackacre.

Under the facts of this case, if *DST*'s trustee has additional powers under the trust agreement such as the power to do one or more of the following: (i) dispose of Blackacre and acquire new property; (ii) renegotiate the lease with Z or enter into leases with tenants other than Z; (iii) renegotiate or refinance the obligation used to purchase Blackacre; (iv) invest cash received to profit from market fluctuations; or (v) make more than minor non-structural modifications to Blackacre not required by law, *DST* will be a business entity which, if it has two or more owners, will be classified as a partnership for federal tax purposes, unless it is treated as a corporation under § 7704 or elects to be classified as a corporation under § 301.7701-3. In addition, because the assets of *DST* will not be owned by the beneficiaries as coowners under state law, *DST* will not be able to elect to be excluded from the application of subchapter K. *See* § 1.761-2(a)(2)(i).

HOLDINGS

(1) The Delaware statutory trust described above is an investment trust, under § 301.7701-4(c), that will be classified as a trust for federal tax purposes.

(2) A taxpayer may exchange real property for an interest in the Delaware statutory trust described above without recognition of gain or loss under § 1031, if the other requirements of § 1031 are satisfied.

EFFECT ON OTHER REVENUE RULINGS

Rev. Rul. 78-371 and Rev. Rul. 92-105 are distinguished.

The principal author of this revenue ruling is Christopher L. Trump of the Office of Associate Chief Counsel (Passthroughs and Special Industries). For further information regarding this revenue ruling, contact Christopher L. Trump at (202) 622-3070 (not a toll-free call).

What is a CCIM?: CCIMs Explained

When choosing a realtor or investment advisor, consider looking for someone who is a Certified Commercial Investment Member (CCIM). This endorsement is bestowed by the Chicago-based CCIM Institute (an affiliate of the National Association of REALTORS) to real estate agents and other professionals who have completed a rigorous 160-hour program of study, including creating a portfolio highlighting their competence in the field of commercial real estate, and passing a comprehensive exam that demonstrates a thorough understanding of ethics, interest-based negotiation, financial analysis, and investment analysis for commercial real estate. Most CCIMs have over two decades of experience in their field of expertise, and this endorsement recognizes a practitioner's dedication to excellence in the profession.

Though CCIMs operate worldwide, they only account for about six percent of all commercial realtors. This small group conducts transactions totaling more than $200 billion annually. CCIMs also average forty-two percent more transactions than the average broker. When you engage the services of a CCIM professional, you're also tapping into a global network of proprietary tools such as listing platforms, statistics and other technology that will give you an edge in securing your deal.

The majority of CCIM professionals are agents or brokers, but leasing professionals, property managers, bankers, investment counselors, attorneys and developers may earn the CCIM affiliation too. CCIMs are dependable, reliable, and have impeccable results-based track records. I recommend selecting a CCIM for your commercial real-estate needs. There are over 13,000 CCIM affiliates out there to deliver exceptional results for you.

LEED Accredited Professional BD&C?

LEED AP BD+C Certification

LEED-certified buildings indicate a project has met specific guidelines in the construction or renovation of a building, and is considered by many in the industry as the gold standard in sustainable development and innovation. As a potential investor, you should be familiar with the terminology surrounding these requirements because a LEED-certified building could be an attractive investment option for your portfolio.

Here's a quick rundown on what you need to know.

LEED-Certified Professionals

LEED, or "Leadership in Energy and Environmental Design," is an internationally-recognized third-party certification program organized and implemented by the U.S. Green Building Council (USGBC). Within the LEED sphere there are different types of credentials, each with specific requirements that address various types of certification. There are five LEED rating systems, covering subsets such as interior design, construction and neighborhood development. These ratings may be applied to projects and professionals.

We're focusing on LEED Accredited Professional Building, Design and Construction (LEED AP BD+C) certification. This certification recognizes professionals—builders, contractors, designers, and architects—who have successfully passed the LEED AP BD+C exam. Those planning construction in commercial, residential, education, and retail spaces are appropriate candidates for this accreditation. Working with a professional who is LEED AP BD+C certified highlights a commitment to the green building movement, and has the potential to increase the value of the building and your investment.

LEED BD+C Certified Projects

Just as people can be accredited LEED professionals by the USGBC, projects are also eligible for LEED credentials. (Within each certification, four levels of certification thresholds determine how "green" a project is.) The following market sectors can benefit from LEED BD+C certification:

- **Healthcare**
  Hospitals providing round-the-clock healthcare, inpatient treatment, and long-term care are eligible.
- **Retail**
  Restaurants, banks, and apparel stores benefit from a LEED-certified project.
- **Schools**
  Just about any learning space on a K-12 campus is eligible, as well as non-academic buildings, like gymnasiums and cafeterias.

- **Hospitality**
  Service industry businesses like motels and hotels maximize their space and their bottom lines by seeking LEED BD+C certification.

- **New Construction**
  LEED can also be applied to building modifications such as HVAC improvements.

Warehouses, data and distribution centers are also potential LEED beneficiaries. LEED AP BD+C certification is revolutionizing contemporary living spaces. For further information, including all application deadlines and fees, consult www.USGBC.org.